5.0 out of 5 Stars

"This book is an excellent review something more than the mate... .... *spiritual waters. It is also a story of hope and a lighthouse for those lost in the storms of spirit to the safe haven prepared for us by our Lord. If you are spiritual, but not religious, you must read this."*
Stephen Roan, Review on Amazon, 10/1/12

Engrossing, well-written, thoughtful, helpful,

"First, this is a story well-told. I disagree with another reviewer who stated that some of the writing was awkward in the beginning of the book. I did not find it so. I was sufficiently engrossed in the story to finish the entire book within two days of purchasing it. There are many, many people whose childhood did not provide them with a satisfying religious experience within Christianity and it is not surprising that such people search for truth in other traditions. I think this author's experience would be invaluable for people attracted to Hinduism, New Age and the occult. The author spent many years involved in New Age and Hindu spiritualism and can speak with the authority of substantial experience. Excellent read, I would recommend it to anyone interested in the interface between Eastern Religions, New Age and Christianity."
By Orianna on Amazon, 1/1/2013

5.0 out of 5 stars
An Inspiring, Open, and Non-Judgmental Account of a Woman's Journey, From New Age Spirituality to the Orthodox Church

"...I read this book in less than two days. It brought me to the verge of tears at several points. I think it will be helpful to many people, especially to women. I especially appreciate the heroic level of honesty with which she openly shares all of her fears, pains, and insecurities along her journey; this brings a level of genuineness to her work not easily found elsewhere. I also very much appreciate that even though she eventually concluded that much of what she had engaged in before her conversion was wrong, and some of it even demonic, that she nevertheless presented these experiences as stepping stones on her journey to Orthodoxy and showed a real appreciation for the ways in which God had reached out to her through those experiences."
By Chris, Massachusetts, USA, 6/1/2012

A truly fascinating read.

"*Veronica Hughes keeps the story moving at a good pace, while still managing to share the basic details of her far-ranging spiritual path, the path, as the subtitle explains, "of a new age seeker to the Light of Christ and the Eastern Orthodox Church." As a pastor in need of awareness of what those who approach me may have experienced in their own pasts, I marveled at the mish-mash world of New Age practices that are so often melded with historical Far Eastern/Oriental religious practices. Hughes reveals much that I was only vaguely aware of before, but, thankfully, without so much detail that the reader might fall prey to an unhealthy fascination with that which she herself left behind. Indeed, she does a remarkable job being kind-hearted toward her past while steadily drawing the reader forward the true Light she eventually found in Christ through Orthodoxy.*"
By Fr. Joseph Bittle, 5/20/2013
Holy Trinity Orthodox Church, Little Rock, AK

"*Author Veronica Hughes takes the reader on a fast-paced wild ride through the world of spirituality. A baby-boomer seeker, she ventures from Roman Catholicism, Hinduism, Buddhism, and a host of other New-Age religious schools and metaphysical movements to the Eastern Orthodox Church. It's basically her life story as the child of an Italian immigrant, baptized into Catholicism, marrying early in life, and pursuing different forms of spirituality to provide healing. Along the way she becomes an educator and authority in channeling messages from ascended masters. After various disappointments and depression, she finds her spiritual home in Christian Orthodoxy. An enjoyable read, I highly recommend it. I notice she also has a website containing some useful resources. Thank you for sharing your story Veronica and I look forward to your next book.*"
By Pierian on Amazon, 5/16/2012

"*Dear Veronica: I have read your book. It was as if you had written my own story. I understood every word on a truly deep and personal level... and like you, I came to the same conclusion by the Grace of God. I became Orthodox a few years ago. Glory to Thee, O God, Glory to Thee! Thank you for writing the book, and for helping those of us who have walked this journey to understand it even more. I hope it will also help those who love others who are walking this same way. May God bless you, now and ever and unto ages of ages.*" By Anna
S. 1/3/2011

The Pearl of Great Price

The Spiritual Journey
of a New Age Seeker to the
Light of Christ and
the Eastern Orthodox Church

Veronica Hughes

The Pearl of Great Price, the Spiritual Journey of a New Age Seeker to the Light of Christ and the Eastern Orthodox Church Third Edition, 2020

Published by:
Pearl Orthodox Christian Publishing
pearlofgreatpriceorthodox.com
email: thepearlofgreatprice@yahoo.com

1/22/23

To my husband, Gregory,
For his enduring love and patience with me.

Table of Contents

Introduction xi

Acknowledgments..xiii

Foreword...xv

Part I
My Labyrinth 1

Chapter 1
Seeking a Better Life in America 3

Chapter 2
My Childhood..9

Chapter 3
"Wait and See" 13

Chapter 4
"You Need to Broaden Your Spiritual Horizons" 20

Chapter 5
The Blue Light..25

Chapter 6
Spiritual Healer and Channel 29

Chapter 7
Unexpected Events 34

Chapter 8
Chance Meetings 39

Chapter 9
India 45

Chapter 10
Completions...53

Chapter 11
Tibetan Buddhism and My "Essence Twin" 58

Chapter 12
Ascended Masters and Initiations of the Soul 62

Chapter 13
Second Chances 66

Chapter 14
From Confusion to Clarity 70

Part II
The Battle for My Soul **79**

Chapter 1
Greg's Epiphany 81

Chapter 2
My Initial Struggles with Eastern Orthodox Christianity 89

Chapter 3
Auschwitz – "The Turning Point" 95

Chapter 4
I reach the center of my Labyrinth 99

Chapter 5
Oh no! Am I becoming one of them? 103

Chapter 6
Walking a Narrow Path 108

Chapter 7
Temptations 114

Part III
My Conversion **117**

Chapter 1
What is Conversion? Who is God? 118

Chapter 2
The Prodigal Daughter Returns 124

Chapter 3
My Baptism. 126

Chapter 4
A duck out of water 129

Chapter 5
The Healing Medicine of Eastern Orthodox Christianity 132

Chapter 6
"The Fall" 135

Chapter 7
Amazing Grace.. 138

Chapter 8
Great Lent 142

Chapter 9
"Have mercy on me, oh God, have mercy on me". 145

Chapter 10
Sickness of Soul..148

Chapter 11
My Soul Wakes Up! 152

Chapter 12
"Why are we here again?" 155

Chapter 13
The Cross 159

Chapter 14
Pascha 163

Epilogue
Then what happened? 167

The End... 167

Appendix I – Setting the record straight about Mary........... 169

Endnotes.. 179

Introduction

"O Lord, you search me and you know me. You know my resting and my rising. You discern my purpose from afar. You mark when I walk or lie down, all my ways lie open to you... O where can I go from your Spirit, or where can I flee from your face?" (Ps. 139:1-3,7)

The words of the psalm do not speak of a "fear-inspiring omnipresence," but of the loving care of someone who looks after us at all times. God sees us in our most hidden places and loves us with a divine mercy. His love is an everlasting love. Veronica's (Polly's) journey, as a New Age seeker, leads to Christ. Her dialogues with God, her husband, and her inner child allow us to watch faith take hold and grow. Faith is always a gift and in it we learn the "greatness and reliability of God's love." Fr. Peter van Breemen reminds of the condition necessary to be able to recognize our own unique call and remain free from distractions. It is impossible unless we "surrender ourselves completely to God's Love." He reminds us that "faith is always an invitation to cross borders, to take advantage of the opening in a horizon that has become too constricting. How many are the borders which faith opens to me! There is, first of all, the call of faith to cross the narrow borders of my own concepts of God. In place of the limited, myopic view I have of God, faith teaches me of his vastness, his transcendence."

She comes to realize that "it was not through our guides, personal will, spiritual prowess or degree of enlightenment that healing had occurred…any healing that occurred from our work together was solely the result of God's compassion and love for us." The knowledge that God continued to love her so unselfishly in spite of her "spiritual arrogance and lack of love, gratitude and awareness of him" revealed to her that the gift of faith that she was receiving was allowing her to know herself accepted by God as she was. She could then accept herself as she was.

Again, I draw from Fr. Peter's insight regarding faith and self-acceptance: "genuine self-acceptance is an act of faith. Even though it may be feared that this kind of faith which leads to self-acceptance will put an end to all striving and desire for change... nothing could be more untrue. On the contrary, the more fully we accept ourselves, the more successfully we can change ourselves. Love is a far better stimulus than threat or pressure.

Veronica stood before the cross of Christ many times before. This time was different. Here, before the image of the crucified Christ, a realization grows that, with confidence, we can ask for the grace of true self-knowledge, which will dispel once and for all any identity crisis. We see the price God has paid for us and understand our worth in the eyes of God with a little more clarity than before. Since God did not spare his own Son, but gave him up to benefit us all, we may be certain, after such a gift, that he will not refuse anything he can give. (Rom 8:32)

"The kingdom of heaven is like a merchant in search of fine pearls, who, on finding one pearl of great value, went and sold all that he had and bought it."

(Mt 13:46)
Glory to God for His mercy and love!

Mat. Elaine Meholick

Acknowledgments

Glory to God for all things!

I wish to thank my editors Ginny Nieswsma and Gayle Atkinson for their support and efforts to bring forth the true spirit and quality of my writing. Ginny believed in my Pearl despite how poorly the first draft of my book was written. She gave me wonderful feedback, encouraged and helped me to find my voice as I worked my way through nine drafts and six years of writing. Then Ginny magnified my voice and helped the spirit of the book to sing with her wonderful evangelical background and editing skills.

Gayle had the patience of a saint as we forged our way through the tedious task of editing my Pearl line by line. I would not have made it through my resistance to this process without your wonderful humor!

I also wish to thank all my friends and colleagues who read my book at various stages of its creation. Each person who read my book and gave me feedback helped me to improve my writing and bring more depth to my story and voice to my words.

I thank Met. Jonah, Bishop Benjamin and all the monks from St. Herman of Alaska monastery for their blessings, wise counsel and spiritual support throughout my struggles to write my story.

I wish to thank my pastor Father Stephan and his wife, M. Elaine for their support and spiritual guidance, and all who prayed for me before and during my conversion. Finally, I wish to thank my husband, Greg, for building our cabin in Platina, California, where I could begin to find the quiet and courage to write my story.

Foreword

I am writing this book for those spiritual seekers earnestly desiring an encounter with the living God. On my journey, I meandered through several religions, movements, metaphysical studies and spiritual practices; indeed, the metaphor that best describes the first half of my life's journey is that of walking a labyrinth.[1] When I walked an actual labyrinth in Chartres Cathedral in France in 1983, I was given a short booklet of instructions about how to navigate the circular pathway. However, because (as a lapsed Catholic) the directions[2] were *too Catholic* for me at the time, I did not read them fully. How I wish I had truly read and followed those instructions! How I approached that walk, unfortunately, was how I approached all of my spiritual questions up to that point, which is to say that myself and ego loomed too large for me to discover the presence of God on the path.

I did arrive at the center and felt pleased and relieved; not everyone is able to accomplish this task in the first attempt. As I walked my way back out that day in Chartres, my ego relished the satisfaction of having solved the puzzle, yet at the same time I knew I had missed *"something."* What was the *something* I had missed? If I had read the directions fully, I would have realized that my journey in this labyrinth was not so much intended for self-revelation, but was meant to bring me out of myself, closer to God. I had missed the whole point of the process—hence, my lingering, nagging disappointment.

This would prove to be the spiritual pattern of my life, until one day I realized that no matter how many times I reached what I thought was my spiritual center, I was not truly where I wanted to be because I still wasn't standing in the presence of the living God. Never could I have planned or imagined that my journey as a seeker would lead me to where I am now, or to who I am now. That is why, after years of searching, having arrived at the end of my own solutions and attempts at encountering God, I was willing to say yes to the dramatic choice that confronted me.

But I am getting ahead of myself, so permit me to go back to the beginning. Here is the story of my journey to find my *"Pearl of Great Price."*

Part I
My Labyrinth

Chapter 1

Seeking a Better Life in America

My Italian Roots

My paternal grandfather came to America from Italy in the late 1890s and settled in North Beach, the Italian district of San Francisco. As did many immigrants of his time, he came to America seeking a better life for his family. While I am missing many details of his life, I do know that he survived the great earthquake of 1906. My grandfather worked for twenty long years to be able to bring his family to America. As often as he was able, he would return to Italy to visit his family and nine months after each visit, my grandmother would give birth to another child. Despite the miles between them most of the time, he and my grandmother Angelina produced five children, two boys and three girls.

My father, Manuel, was their youngest child. He was born in 1912 in Velva, a small rural village about one hour away from the Italian Mediterranean. Manuel joined a family that was dirt poor and living in a small house with no plumbing just below the village church. My father later remembered that when my grandfather's fortunes improved in America and he sent money home, the family was able to move across the street to a larger house with a toilet—understandably, a big deal!

In Velva, Father's family raised most of their own vegetables in a garden they shared with neighbors. At times during the winter they did not have enough food. One of my aunts told me that as children they looked forward to the birth of other children, because births in the village, or holy days of the church, were the only times their family ate meat. Frequently, the children went without shoes, and all of them worked from the age of six to help make ends meet, laboring as field hands or carrying wood on their heads for miles.

As time went on, my grandfather arranged for the eldest son, Mario, to come to America first, and as an American he fought in WWI. My father and aunts grew up in Italy during the war, and life was especially difficult for them during this period. Food shortages affected everyone - villagers and prisoners at a nearby POW camp, alike. My aunts often took many risks, as did the other villagers, to secretly bring food to the starving Allied prisoners. If chronic hunger wasn't enough suffering, all my paternal ancestors also managed to survive the flu epidemic that struck Europe and the United States from which at least half their village perished. Life in rural Italy revolved around their local church and the cathedral at the top of the mountain behind them. My aunts would tell me how they walked in processions, carrying icons and statues of Mary, Christ's mother. The family frequently went to Mass, sometimes daily. Because of the proximity of our family to their local church, and the absence of a father, the parish priest occasionally helped to discipline my father and his older brother. An unfortunate consequence of this was that my father resented the intrusion and later avoided both priests and church attendance.

When my grandfather finally arranged to bring the rest of his family to the United States in 1921 on a ship named *America*, they almost perished on their voyage. In later years, my aunt frequently told the story of the harrowing experience tossing and shaking on the ship during a raging storm with hurricane force winds.

The passengers and crew cowered as a thirty-foot wave hit their ship. It broke open the parlor room door where many people, including my family, had gathered for safety. The ship tilted as seawater crashed into the room. My father lost his footing and was just about to be carried overboard when someone grabbed him and saved his life! The crew gave the passengers lifejackets and sent them to their rooms, but my family went to bed that night not knowing if they would survive the storm. All the papers in the United States and in Italy reported that their ship had sunk, but then several days later the *America* sailed into Ellis Island with all safe on board. What a way to start life in America!

Sadly, after my father came to America, he had a strained relationship with his father, whom he met for the first time when he arrived with his sisters and his mother. The separation of years and oceans the family had endured for the sake of a better life in America had taken its toll; my grandfather had become an alcoholic over the course of his time alone. Frequently so drunk that he would spend a night in jail, he would frequently fight with my grandmother.

At the age of sixteen, to escape the hardships of his home life, my dad ran away, became a hobo and rode the rails for a year. Eventually, he notified my worried grandmother and aunts that he was surviving by doing odd jobs, playing pool and gambling. Dad learned to gamble from my grandfather, who almost gambled the family's house away one night when he was drunk. Thank God, the bartender called my grandmother to alert our family, and through his kind intervention, a tragedy was averted.

When my dad finally returned home, he settled into the family business of selling flowers on the street. My grandfather had opened his first flower stand in front of the first Bank of Italy, which later became the Bank of America.

Throughout his bachelor years, my father frequently took risks, living dangerously and gambling, winning and losing fortunes on the same night. At night, peddling flowers on Tin Pan Alley, he would often meet famous entertainers of his time, including George Gershwin. True to character, my father didn't marry until he was forty-two years old, but when he married my mother, he was finally ready to settle down.

My Irish, Swiss, and German Roots

My mother's father, Carl, was Swiss and German. His family came to the United States in the late 1800s and settled in Oakland, California. Carl became an electrician and built his own business, which he lost (as many did) during the Great Depression. To make ends meet, he picked up odd jobs, one of which was his stint as an electrician on the Golden Gate Bridge.

My mother recounted to me how my grandfather came home quite shaken after witnessing the historic and fatal accident of sixteen men who fell to their deaths. After this trauma, Grandfather Carl never went back to work on the bridge, and he also began to drink more heavily.

My maternal grandmother, Frances, was Irish and grew up in Oakland as well. Frances's parents knew Jack London before he became famous. The writer would frequently show up for my great- grandmother's home cooking, and over dinner would share the stories that later made him famous. Grandmother Frances became a nurse and began her nursing career during the devastating flu epidemic in 1917. She went on to become one of the first nurses to work privately for a physician in San Francisco.

My mother, Roberta, was born in 1925 in Oakland. After a few years her parents settled in the North Beach area of The City (as San Francisco was called) on Chestnut Street. Unlike my father, who grew up in a large Italian family, my mom was an only child. As did all the children of the '20s and '30s, mother grew up during the Depression and her family struggled to make ends meet. My grandmother's nursing profession saved them from utter poverty when my grandfather could not find work. My mother remembers that they frequently fed strangers that would knock on their door looking for food or handouts. During these years, mother contracted rheumatic fever in her early teens and fought to recover for more than a year. She was fortunate to survive the illness, which killed so many others.

My mom was a consummate shopper and smart dresser; due to the material deprivation she endured as a child, she resolved that she would always be able to live by the motto: "When the going gets tough, the tough go shopping!" Hard working and independent, my mother joined the Coast Guard in 1943, lying about her age so she could enlist. While she wanted to do her duty, she also yearned to get away from home and see the world. Mother married a young naval man who served on the battleship "Arizona" and had fortunately survived the attack on Pearl Harbor. Following a whirlwind romance and wedding, they both went on active duty. They did not see each other again until after the war ended. While my mother did not "see the world", she did get as far as New York City.

She enjoyed serving as an administrative assistant there until the war ended. Her first marriage fell apart shortly after reuniting with her husband. Single once again, my mother chose to attend UC Berkeley, thanks to the GI Bill, where she earned her bachelor's degree.

My parents frequently talked about their unique relationship, which began long before they fell in love. They had known each other when my mom was a child. Seventeen years older than my mother, dad would see mom playing in their neighborhood. Often they waved and said hello to each other, and he knew her parents. In the late 1940s, my father opened a flower shop on the corner of Greenwich and Columbus Avenues in the heart of North Beach. Soon after, my mom became sick and someone had ordered flowers for her, which my dad delivered, and they renewed their acquaintance as adults. My mom said she was "swept off her feet" by my father who delivered not one, but two dozen roses to her doorstep. Sparks flew, followed by their courtship and marriage in 1951. Mom also started working in the flower shop with my dad. San Franciscans called North Beach, *The Little City*, so our flower shop was named *Little City Florist*.

The hardships both my parents endured during their childhood- -the Depression and World War II—shaped them in different ways. Wanting to fulfill his needs for financial stability and independence, my street-wise father was not averse to risk-taking, which later was tempered by family responsibilities. Through the years of selling flowers, he developed a wonderful way of complimenting and relating to his customers and people in general. The rough life my father had lived taught him how to roll with the punches. If angry, dad would briefly explode but then it was over, and he excelled at letting go of resentments, debts and worries. He chose to see the good in others and let go of the rest, so much so that towards the end of his life, I rarely heard him say an unkind word about anyone.

My mother accomplished her goals with more subtlety. For her, working equaled freedom from poverty, and independence – so my mother always made sure she worked and had money of her own to spend on whatever she wanted. Spirited, attractive, talented artistically and well educated, she grappled with how to accept and forgive hurts, unresolved debts or resentments. Her mother, Frances, and her sister, Florence, didn't speak to each other for thirty years, which had lasting effect on my mother, who believed that no hurt was worth that kind of alienation, and she consequently struggled with how to find peace with her emotions and pains throughout her own life. As hard as my mother tried, depression and physical pain related to her past struggles haunted her at times; in spite of her pain, however, she pushed through personal loss and tragedy with great courage and patience. Towards the end of her life, my mother's deepening faith in God and her innate loving and playful personality helped her to finally overcome her inner demons. She became a radiant light of courage to us all. Her final words to each family member on her last day were, "I love you."

My family's history, struggles and accomplishments as they sought a better life in America shaped me, and in a sense, my seeker's journey began even before my birth. Taking risks, my family triumphed over near-death experiences, abject poverty, the Depression and two world wars. This would be my birthright and inheritance as I began my sojourn in this place and time.

Chapter 2

My Childhood

On January 6, 1953, the Feast of Epiphany in the Catholic Church, and Theophany in the Orthodox tradition, I was born in San Francisco, California and named Paula Angela Sivori. About a year before I was born, my parents endured the heartache of the loss of their first-born child, a son, to a stillbirth. My mom was terrified that she would lose me as well; thus, when I was born alive and kicking, my parents experienced such joy! As a child, Epiphany to me meant "little Christmas," the day the Magi brought their gifts to Christ. Since every year, twelve days after Christmas, I received my birthday gifts the same day Christ had received His, I always insisted my parents keep our Christmas tree up until at least January 7.

My grandmother Angelina died in my first year of life, so I have no memories of her, but I was always told she had a lovely voice, which I inherited. She and my aunts wanted the children in our family to be baptized Catholic. While my parents believed in God, they were not religious—my father seldom went to church and my mother's family raised her in a nominally religious upbringing as a Protestant. Yet they wanted to honor the wishes of my dying grandmother, and so after my sister Carla was born on March 10, 1955, both of us were baptized.

We lived in the lower flat of my aunt's North Beach house, and my father's sister, Aunt Lena lived upstairs. My devout, observant Aunt oversaw our religious upbringing. Aunt Lena insisted that my sister and I attend church with her frequently in our early years; she herself went to Mass daily before reporting for work at the cracker factory. For my aunts, as with many Italian village Catholics, spiritual contradictions lived side by side. Aunt Lena dabbled in tea leaf, card and palm readings and on her breaks at work, she'd read her friends' fortunes. Before she left Italy, she had consulted a fortuneteller who assured her that she would have enough money and live a long, good life in America. (My aunt lived to be 98.) This blend of Catholic tradition and rural superstition influenced me and from an early age, I was accustomed to dabbling in the occult.

Work and family life were one in the same in our family. In those days, my parents adhered to a strict budget. My mother could not afford a basinette for me so she used gardenia boxes to carry me back and forth to work when I was a baby. People from Italy gathered daily in our flower shop to reminisce about the old country while eating dried bread dipped in coffee. Everyone was welcome. North Beach was a large village and as children we felt safe there. Cable cars went by our store and rang their bells. Across the street from our flower shop, the library, playground and community pool beckoned, and Fisherman's Wharf was only a few blocks away. We lived on famous Telegraph Hill and often played in the parking lot of the Coit Tower. I loved our colorful, Italian neighborhood with its wonderful pastry shops and restaurants where everyone knew each other.

An adventurous little girl with a tomboy streak, I sometimes fancied myself the son my father never had, and until I started school, I was his constant companion. By my fifth birthday, our little house in North Beach had become too small for our growing family and we moved to a much bigger house in the Sunset District of San Francisco, right next to Golden Gate Park. At six years of age, I started public school and within a year I found trouble. Picking a fight with a bully to defend a boy who was my friend, I won! Later, I decided to lie to my parents so I could visit this same friend at his house after school. I told my parents that I had to stay after school to do "special homework." Unfortunately, I did not factor in my mother phoning the school at 4 p.m. because I had not yet returned home. When she discovered that I wasn't and that there was no such thing as "special homework," she frantically called the police.

Meanwhile, by five p.m. my young friend's mother finally figured out that something was amiss. She thought it odd that I had invited myself to dinner! As soon as she called my mother, I knew my good time had ended. Did I catch hell for that! I was truly my father's daughter. After those incidents, my parents decided it was time to put both my sister and me in a Catholic school, in the hope that I would calm down and get a better education, a prescient and significant decision. When I entered St. Bridget's Catholic School from public school, I skipped a grade and crammed two years of learning into one. My mom and I spent our afternoons and weekends going over my homework, and I remember singing my times tables for hours to memorize them. When I passed third grade, a seemingly impossible goal, both of us rejoiced in the achievement and we bonded more deeply through working towards our mutual goal. That year I also learned how to fit in with older children by pretending that I knew more than I really did; this coping skill proved invaluable, but was also one of my downfalls as I matured.

Our school and church were next door to each other, which enabled me to attend mass regularly, sometimes even daily. I liked being in church. I often would go there before and after school, sitting quietly, not really knowing exactly what I was doing, but experiencing nonetheless a deep sense of peace and Presence. It is difficult to describe my first spiritual awakening at the age of nine. Our nuns sponsored a retreat in the quiet woods and mountains of Northern California in the early fall. Part of this retreat focused on Mary, the Mother of Jesus; the sisters also directed our young minds towards the concept of repentance. They explained that the derivation of the word comes from the Old French "repentir": re, in response to, and pentir, to be sorry.

Following the instructions of the nuns for the weekend, I asked Mary for help and earnestly sought God's forgiveness, as only a child can do. Shortly thereafter, alone in their beautiful little chapel, I quietly prayed to Christ and His Mother. At some point during my prayer, a soft, sweet Light touched me and held me in its embrace, suspending time and space. I do not remember any words, but I experienced a soft voice speaking to my heart and soul, and I wept with both joy and sorrow. Even though I was only a child, the overwhelming sense of love, compassion and peace that embraced me in that Light was as real as anything I've ever known. Warmth flooded my whole body, my heart felt aflame with love for Mary, and this feeling stayed with me when I returned home. Filled with this love and longing, I fell asleep that night dreaming of a life devoted to God as a nun.

When I returned home, I enthusiastically told my mother what had happened. At first she listened to my story with approval, until I told her that I had decided to become a nun. At a loss for how to respond or what to say, she heard me out, but with a changed countenance. She thought she had sent me to a benign Catholic camp! Ultimately, she concluded that my newfound zeal was a childish phase. As was true for many other parents, she was simply unable to understand a religious calling that would alter her life as well as mine. Like most mothers, she wanted me to get married and live a traditional lifestyle. "Wait for a while and see what happens, dear." Through my tears, I insisted, "But mom, you don't understand. I feel called. I want this more than anything". She replied, "Let's wait and see, okay? You don't know how you will feel when you get older." She kissed me good night and said "We will discuss this later."

From that point on, I would periodically bring the subject up, hopeful that she would allow me to pursue my spiritual desire for monasticism. I wanted to go on other meditative retreats, but mom avoided them, sending me instead to Catholic Youth camp. She betted on the forgetfulness of youth, and as time passed, I realized that I was not going to be allowed to become a nun. Disappointed, my spiritual awakening faded and the warmth in my heart and soul cooled. Life went on, but something had changed in me. Sadness and bitterness replaced my ardor, and in one of my life's defining phases, I began to unconsciously befriend and incline myself towards holding onto resentments and judgments. I closed a door and started my journey away from God.

Chapter 3

"Wait and See"

Someone once said to me that "When you wait, and when you don't choose, life or someone will choose for you." "Wait and see" now began to choose the direction of my life. As I approached my early teenage years, the Catholic Church was changing too. I had loved the ritual and depth of the services before Vatican II, but after the council, most Catholic churches shortened the Mass. Despite the fact that I liked hearing the words of the service in English, something was missing for me - church did not move me and bring me towards God as it had when I was a child.

As I matured, I began to dislike attending both Catholic school and Mass. I could never escape the feeling of guilt and my sense of sin trapped and suffocated me. As a member of the *Baby Boomer* generation, and as the daughter of hard-working parents, I didn't suffer from physical deprivation, but from spiritual poverty. For all our material comforts, my life was still a struggle, and I often felt at odds with the world and my moody, rebellious and ungrateful teenaged self.

Around me, "the times, they were a changing" too. My generation protested the Vietnam War and celebrated sex without commitment and the liberal use of drugs. But we also aspired to live up to the words and actions of Bobby Kennedy and Martin Luther King, Jr. Their assassinations when I was in high school devastated my generation and dealt a lethal blow to our naïve, but well-intentioned, idealism and hope. My anger and apathy increased after their lives were so brutally snuffed out. Truth and beauty, however, did find a way into my heart through books and music. By the age of twenty, I had read J.R. Tolkein's *Lord of the Rings* series four times, captivated by allegorical portrayals of the struggle between good and evil. Deep in my soul, I clung to the belief in the existence of Good, even while losing much of my hope in the power of Good to change the world. Tolkein's novels inspired my hope that a new age would be birthed through the triumph of good over evil by the efforts of seemingly insignificant people, such as the little hobbits of Tolkein's imagination. I loved escaping into his magical world. Other works of art inspired me also, such as Tchaikovsky's music and great English novels such as *Jane Eyre* and *Tale of Two Cities*. I adored classic love stories and as a hopeless romantic, always rooted for the underdog and a happy ending.

Just before entering college when I was seventeen years old, my mom and I were in an automobile accident. As was typical in the 1960s, neither of us was wearing seatbelts at the time. Another vehicle hit us just behind my passenger seat and our van rolled over three times and was completely totaled. The inside of our van was metal and I can still recall the crunching sound as we rolled. I was thrown to the back and ricocheted back and forth, every part of my body hitting the car's interior multiple times. My mom stayed in her seat thanks to the steering wheel, and by the grace of God we avoided death! That car accident, coupled with a skiing accident several years later, would eventually be the start of a whole new chapter in my life - my struggle with physical pain. However, at the age of seventeen, I did not worry about the potential long-term consequences of anything, including the depth of my physical injuries.

After the accident, my mom became interested in yoga. Our recent accident had left its mark on both of us. For mother, it had aggravated her chronic back pain. She decided it would be good for us to take a yoga class together. This was my first taste of Eastern meditation combined with movement and breathing. Yoga calmed my mind and eased the tensions in my body, helping me to step out of my emotional and physical pain. Our yoga teacher seemed to live in a peaceful and calm world. Her statues of Hindu gods and goddesses all around her studio reminded me of the statues in the Catholic Church, as did her incense and candles. The difference was that there were no rules about states of sin in yoga, and I didn't have to agonize over my shortcomings. The spirituality in yoga made me feel better and came without guilt!

I had high hopes when I entered college and declared French to be my major course of study and geology my minor. I was accustomed to earning As in French in both high school and my first year in college. In the first semester of my second year, I took a course with a tough French professor. Even with the help of a tutor, I could not pull higher than a C and at the end of the semester, my professor confronted me. He told me that I would never make a good French teacher and that I should do something else. I was devastated and disillusionment set in. His blunt, uncaring assessment offered me neither hope nor options, and his words shattered my youthful dreams and goals.

In the meantime, I fell in love. My boyfriend was demanding of my time, strongly opinionated and independent, and challenged me to grow up. An art major and artist, Peter beautified my world as he showered me with his creations. What's more, my parents, whose opinions mattered to me, not only liked him, but my father essentially adopted him as the son he'd always wanted.

What next? Uninspired by college, I dropped out after two years of study, found a job at a pharmacy, and set out on the only path that seemed available to me, marriage. At the age of twenty, in spite of our aversion to tradition, Peter and I announced our engagement. We wanted to get married in Golden Gate Park but my fiancée's mother, a traditional Polish Catholic, wouldn't hear of it, so we consented to a wedding at St. Stephen's Catholic Church. I did, however, make sure that my bridesmaids wore pantsuits and I refused to wear an expensive dress. At our reception, due to our tight budget, our food disappeared in the first ten minutes! I was mortified. Italian and Polish families excel at providing large quantities of good food for their guests. Additionally, the sound system failed during our first dance. Thank God for the champagne and cake, of which we had plenty! Most of our older relatives and guests became quite inebriated – especially the Irish side of the family. In the end, all the guests went home happy, but not so the bride. Ever the discontented idealist, I kept replaying each faux pas and crying throughout the first week of our honeymoon. Thus, began my marriage.

My new husband and I bought a mobile home in Colma, California, outside of San Francisco. For our livelihood, we joined my dad in a family partnership and opened two outdoor flower stands. My dad and Peter worked well together, and for the next few years my life revolved around my husband, our flower stands and our families.

I grew up in the '50s and '60s, watching family television shows such as *Leave it to Beaver*, the *Donna Reed Show*, and *My Three Sons*. Week after week, I absorbed the portrayal of perfect marriages and ideal families. My Baby Boomer generation expected life to be as it was portrayed was on TV – perfect, except for a few ups and downs that we cheerfully accepted, knowing there would be a happy ending in a half an hour! Why was this version of life not quite working for me? I was 20 years old and was straining to be the perfect wife in the perfect marriage. The 'great cook' part I learned pretty quick, but the 'at home wife with children' part was not happening and in fact, terrified me. Neither of us desired to become parents quickly.

I pushed myself to conform to what my husband wanted. I had an image in my mind about what I should do to achieve my perfect marriage, and how I would feel then, and how we would interact and live as a married couple. I was supposed to feel more in love with my husband after following my 'perfect marriage model' formula. Instead, by our second wedding anniversary, my husband and I had already begun to argue frequently. More than once while we were playing tennis, I had become so infuriated that I threw down my racket and stormed off the tennis court, in tears over something Peter had said. Why was my husband so critical, I fumed? Peter was an extremely competitive, natural athlete. I, on the other hand, lacked physical stamina, no matter how much I worked out and struggled to keep up with him. I wanted to compete with him and win. Impossible! We were both emotionally immature and strong willed, a deadly combination. As time passed and the frictions between us continued, I fell into a deepening depression.

During this phase of our marriage, I started receiving a massage once a week, seeking relief not only from the pain in my back and body, but also in my heart and soul. Frequently shrouded in fog for days at a time, Colma weather depressed me, and so did my critical husband.

Another form of relief came through flirtatious interactions with other men, and more than once I entertained the temptation of starting an affair with men who found me attractive. Ultimately, I resisted and confessed my desires to my husband which, while relieving my guilt, increased the stress and lack of trust between us.

In the midst of this marriage strain, our career direction and financial situation radically changed when the leases on both of our flower stands came up for renewal. Our landlord demanded a large rent increase and my dad responded by deciding to retire. I obtained another position as a pharmacy clerk, which I thought would be a good job. Unfortunately, my boss was an angry alcoholic, and before long I felt trapped in a miserable job.

Looking for better ways to earn money, my husband decided to open a stained-glass business. We both had dabbled in stained glass as a hobby while running the flower stands, and after years of mentoring with my father about how to run a small business, my husband thought he could succeed. We lacked, however, my father's financial resources and his years of business experience and connections. We were also choosing a completely different line of work. We had to learn how to design and create salable, competitively priced, original art, and then find buyers. Completely out of money, we sold our mobile home and moved in with my parents, and their basement became our studio.

By this point, any illusions I had about my perfect marriage had perished in the realities of our daily lives. Also, during this time, my old accident injury flared up, and my back pain became so excruciating that I was not able to sit comfortably for any length of time. After experiencing a miscarriage and a bout of colitis, I became increasingly desperate for a way to improve my life. Physically, I could not continue to work at the pharmacy. Relieved – but now out of work - I signed up to collect unemployment benefits.

At this point, when I was as open as I had ever been to new solutions, a friend introduced me to *EST* (Erhard Seminars Training), a personal growth process very popular in the 70s. After an introductory guest event, I decided I wanted to go to a weekend workshop, but I wasn't sure how to bring up the subject with my husband. One night, I opened my heart to my mom about EST, my discouragement about life and my desire to change myself. We attended a seminar together in the hope that we would both improve our lives and relationship, which had become compromised by our living under the same roof. Both my dad and husband thought we were slightly crazy, but agreed to let us go.

A product of Zen Buddhism and 70s spirituality, our first workshop taught mom and me some worthwhile life and relationship skills. To this day, I attribute our ability to engage in healthy communication with each other to our efforts that began in EST. As I participated in more programs offered by EST, I began to understand the roots of my depression. Instead of trying to be a perfect wife and daughter, I learned that I needed to take responsibility for my actions and for how I communicated with others. Encouraged in my newfound knowledge, I insisted that my husband attend a seminar, and with tremendous resistance and after several intense arguments, Peter finally consented. Mercifully, our first seminar together helped him too, and offered both of us tools that we needed as a young couple. Putting our new skills to work, we began to fight less and connect more emotionally.

Undeterred by the controversy surrounding EST and its handsome and charismatic founder, Werner Erhardt, we quickly joined the ranks of true EST believers. My friends and I were ready to do just about anything for Werner and 'the work'. Werner was an eloquent speaker, playing to packed crowds at the Oakland Coliseum, as well as a competent, shrewd businessman. His techniques and lifestyle challenged the norms of our times and people considered his workshops to be groundbreaking.

EST seminars had nothing to do with religion, but they did allow me to reach for something higher in life than my relationship with my husband. We both needed to mature, for our relationship was selfish, and it was suffocating both of us. Stepping out of ourselves and reaching for something greater, we started to volunteer in our local EST office. EST promoted the idea that we could truly make a difference in the world and change what was not working. This gave us a sense of renewed purpose. Since I felt somewhat of a failure in my attempt to pursue higher learning in college, I also jumped at the chance to prove myself, and so I stayed with EST for seven years, participating in every program they offered, sometimes more than once.

EST would be the first of many movements I would join over the course of my spiritual journey. Why did I embrace each movement so wholeheartedly and steadfastly? Part of my commitment sprang from my gratitude for the positive changes that I experienced in my life as a result of what I learned in each movement. I would become involved because I wanted to give something back in return for the things that I had received. Growing up hearing about my family's struggles in a new country, I had always valued the virtues of loyalty and thankfulness.

However, at the deepest level, I plunged into each movement with my heart and soul because I kept hoping that I could find inner peace and be connected to something greater than myself. I kept looking for the food that would satisfy my inner spiritual hunger. Each program I tried, each movement I joined, helped me for a time, as I would work my way through my life's maze, one dysfunctional behavior at a time. Ultimately, however, I would become discontent, depressed and restless with each movement - something was missing - yet I would resist the need to move on. I would often stay involved just to please others, hoping to gain their love and respect, or sometimes I would feel guilty for wanting to leave. Thus, I often stayed too long in unhealthy personal or professional relationships, committed to movements or programs I no longer truly embraced. Eventually, the pressure to exit would build, my body would sicken, and I would wrestle with a feeling of malaise until a change, often accompanied by anger or resentment, erupted from me like a volcano. Shocked and unprepared, the people in my life often didn't see my discontent brewing. I would even be surprised myself, because I was often blind to the inner workings of my heart.

Now I can look back on those days with greater clarity, but at the time, I believed in each one of these movements that our journey together, through my book, describes. I have tried to tell my story with transparency and without judgment. Each program I participated in was a stepping-stone on the path to my heart's desire. The conclusions I drew from each of my spiritual experiences are how I felt, believed and thought at the time. Some of the lessons I learned along the path remain with me today. Other teachings I questioned and challenged and they didn't survive as I worked my way out of my labyrinth. There would come a time when I began to see my life, choices, beliefs and experiences in a completely different Light, one that would illumine for me all that had transpired over the course of my life. But I am getting ahead of myself once again.

Chapter 4

"You Need to Broaden Your Spiritual Horizons"

When our stained-glass business finally could support us, we moved out of my parents' house to Oakland, a city across the San Francisco Bay. During our first few years there, several life-changing developments occurred simultaneously. First, I became close friends with a woman I met in EST when we volunteered together at our local office. Different from any one I had previously known, Nancy sparkled! Her attributes included contagious enthusiasm and an ability to constructively challenge my ideas and ways of viewing life; she was insightful, not critical. In turn, she found me supportive and accessible, and before long, we both felt that we knew what was in each other's hearts. We became best friends and soul sisters. Th ere was a chemistry between us that neither of us had experienced before.

My husband and I rented an older house in a quiet Oakland neighborhood and set up our stained-glass studio in one of the bedrooms. After about a year there, I became quite ill due to the accumulative years of chemical exposure from our stained-glass business. Entering our studio could cause me to feel nauseated or to throw up. We simply didn't have any awareness then about the health hazards of our profession and the importance of properly managing the toxins. For years, we didn't think about wearing gloves or venting the fumes from the soldering chemicals.

We had a few fans in our workshop but they were not placed with any particular intention. For a while, I thought I had a recurring flu, but I became suspicious about my reactions to the odors in our studio when they began to make me feel ill even from a distance.

At some point, my husband went away for a week-long EST event. While he was away, I began a juice fast to test my theory about our chemicals making me sick. I had read about various forms of fasting in a local health food store and hoped the fast would make me feel better. Instead, after one day I reacted with all the symptoms of a severe flu, chills, vomiting and weakness. Our studio was near our bathroom and simply walking by it, made me vomit. When my husband returned and I described my physical symptoms to him, he was shocked and we were both thrown into turmoil. What would we do if the chemicals we used in our business were, indeed, making me sick? This was our livelihood, after all! One thing I did know: my chemical sensitivities demanded that I find another way to support our household. Peter would have to manufacture and manage our business on his own. I hoped that removing myself from our business would fix the problem.

Nancy was a waitress and helped me find a job waiting tables at The Merritt, a middle-class restaurant in the heart of Oakland. Working at The Merritt was refreshingly common. I loved the interaction with the working-class people of Oakland, and the cooks and single men at the counter flirted and joked with us non-stop. The milieu reminded me, in its own unique way, of my family's flower shop and the easy banter among the folks who gathered there. During each shift, I was swept up into the next episode of our local soap opera/sitcom. My friend and I were able to arrange being scheduled for the same shifts most of the week, which added to my comfort working there. Since I had been working with my husband or in family businesses most of my life, I enjoyed the environment at The Merritt as something different. For the first time in years, I was not spending most of my time with my husband but with my best friend, and this benefitted both relationships. I brought home to my husband not only my hard-earned money, but also great stories and interesting topics for conversation. As we waited tables, we talked about life and one day she ventured, "Polly, you need to broaden your spiritual horizons". "OK", I said, "What do you have in mind?" Nancy pulled out a grocery store list of spiritual venues for us to sample and discuss. We started with astrology, and after individual sessions with her astrologer, we compared notes about our readings and charts. Fascinated, we read our daily horoscopes together to see what fate awaited us that day. Eventually, our conversations expanded from horoscopes to gurus and other spiritual subjects.

During this time, my husband and I purchased a duplex home from a dear family friend. In her early 90s, Mary could no longer climb the stairs or live alone. We were simultaneously thrilled and overwhelmed, for the house needed extensive remodeling. Since Nancy's new husband was a contractor, we hired him for the job. Unfortunately, his work ethic left much to be desired, although when he actually showed up to work, he did a good job. We gave him a six-month time line to ready the upstairs apartment for us.

Our optimistic timeline turned out to be too much for our overscheduled contractor friend; in the middle of winter, we moved into an unfinished unit with no heat, no kitchen, no finished walls except in the bedrooms, and no working master bathroom. Thank God, we had a toilet on our floor and a fully functional bathroom in the lower flat that we could use, and a working fireplace! We ate out every day, living with the dust and the cold for months while we ran out of money and patience. Meanwhile, our contractor kept promising to deliver and kept failing to keep his word. Within a year, Nancy divorced our unreliable contractor and our working relationship with him ended as well.

During this time, I started another physical downhill slide. I had been so caught up in our perpetual house problems that I had failed to start, or even investigate, any treatment for my chemically induced symptoms. Secretly, I had hoped that a change of jobs and the lack of further exposure would magically heal me. In addition to experiencing chronic exhaustion caused by the toxins in my body, I stopped taking birth control pills and had no menstrual cycle. One year after we had moved into our own house, the domino effect of the remodeling disaster and my untreated health problems resulted in another health collapse. My energy level dropped to the point that I couldn't continue to work, even as a waitress. This triggered another depression; each morning I'd wake up hoping that I was having a bad dream rather than stepping into another day of my life. Feeling useless and powerless, I'd sit in our unfinished mess of a home and cry. Tensions between my husband and I returned as we struggled to make ends meet again.

Once again, my spiritually curious friend Nancy came to my rescue. She had been seeing a psychic healer, Becky, and she thought that I could benefit from a session with her, so she gave me the session as a gift. Feeling desperate, I was willing to try anything that might help me feel better. I visited Becky's humble accommodations for a session and felt calmed by her soothing presence and soft smile. I told her about my health problems; she, in turn, introduced me to psychic healing.

Becky relaxed me by directing me through a guided visualization. As I went deeper and deeper into meditation, lulled by Becky's mellow voice, I entered into an altered state of consciousness where I listened to her from a distance, even though she sat only four feet away. Suddenly, I was out of my body and looking down at myself, and Becky's "guides" introduced themselves to me in this disembodied place. We conversed for a time until Becky's voice slowly returned and the guides faded away. My out-of-body experience, combined with the intimacy I felt with her guides, left me speechless. It felt as though healing had occurred within me on a profound level. What happened and how, I was not sure, but I felt changed. At the time, no inner alarm bells went off; in my misery, I could only be grateful for the relief her work brought me.

Becky told me I had a natural talent for psychic healing that she rarely encountered and that I would become a spiritual healer some day. During one of my subsequent sessions, she said that her guides had determined that I had a pre-cancerous condition in my ovaries. They advised me to seek help immediately and to find a physician that practiced alternative medicine. I had encountered so many dead ends with traditional doctors related to my ongoing heath problems that I was ready to try something different. Through a local health food store, I found a referral and made an appointment.

In my first visit, the alternative doctor used a crystal pendulum and muscle testing to diagnose my health problems. For the first time in my life, I felt that a physician was giving me an accurate diagnosis. He could see from his testing that my hormonal system was abnormal. He also told me that I had Chronic Fatigue Syndrome. He explained that even with my depressed immune system and lack of energy, in time I could regain my health. For the first time in years, I had a reason to hope and a new treatment protocol to try.

From analyzing my hair content, the doctor found extraordinarily high levels of lead, copper and other chemicals in my body. Lead poisoning can be lethal and I knew enough to be frightened by what he was telling me. The treatments he proposed were more than challenging. I was to be on a strict vegan diet and consume two 16-ounce glasses of raw carrot and celery juice a day. He prescribed glandular extracts and numerous vitamin supplements, and advised me to start practicing yoga and meditation again to help me calm my mind and energize my body.

Instead of the normal office light rock playing in the background, the doctor played some form of Far Eastern chanting for his patients. Intrigued as always, I asked him about it during my next appointment. Called "Om Nama Shivaya", the chant was sung by the doctor's famous guru, Muktananda, whose photographs hung on the walls throughout his office. My doctor turned out to be the primary care physician for Muktananda, and he encouraged me to purchase the same mantra tape for my use during yoga sessions. I learned later that Werner Erhart, the founder of EST, had brought Muktananda to the United States. They had toured together and several of my friends in EST had become his devotees. This coincidence only increased my spiritual receptivity to the guru and this doctor.

I went home and started my new health and spiritual regime. My husband thought I had gone slightly off the deep end again. My skin turned light orange from all the carrot and celery juice I was drinking and our refrigerator was dominated by a 25-pound bag of carrots. One of the remodeled bedrooms in our house became my meditation and yoga sanctuary and I spent 1-2 hours a day in my special room. The more I chanted while doing yoga with the mantra tape, the deeper I went into my new inner world, and the better I felt when I returned to my real world. In my daily sessions I felt enraptured, as though I were floating on a cloud.

Chapter 5
The Blue Light

After four months of meditating and practicing yoga twice a day, while listening to my mantra tapes, I was surprised to perceive a beautiful blue light which appeared in my mind's eye, a point called the "third eye" in Hinduism. As I continued to chant internally, the blue light expanded. Eventually, my entire internal vision was transfixed on this now pulsating and glowing light. Slowly, the image of a Far Eastern looking older man appeared to me. He reached out and touched me on the area of the third eye, after which my conscious awareness faded into a deep state of trance for at least an hour. When I awoke in a somewhat altered state, I felt healed and enlivened.

I believed that something spiritually significant had happened to me, and wondered if the man who appeared to me was Muktananda; my friend Becky confirmed that he had, indeed, visited me. When I went to Muktananda's ashram, which was not far from my house, to talk with other people about my experience, they exclaimed, "What a great blessing!" They told me that I had experienced a form of internal, long distance Hindu initiation. The guru himself had come and awakened me!

This experience was quite mysterious and exciting to me, and I began to read books written by Muktananda, as well as books about him written by others, to better understand what happened. Knowing next to nothing about Hindu spiritual practices or mysticism, I embarked on my first Eastern spiritual journey, immersing myself into what was now the beginning of spiritual discipline. I bought more mantra tapes. I began going to the ashram on Friday evenings to join their group meditations and watch videos of recent events with Muktananda.

Due to his relationship with Werner Erhart, Muktananda was one of the first gurus to reach out to Westerners during the era when New Age practices and Eastern religions were gaining acceptance and followers in the United States. Prior to my introduction to EST, Werner had brought Muktananda to the United States and had helped him develop a large network of ashrams. Shrewd in his use of the latest media technologies, Werner knew how to kindle a sense of personal connection with Muktananda's devotees, similar to the way he had used these techniques in EST. Additionally, his popularity was enhanced by many rich and famous devotees, such as John Denver, who embraced the guru's teachings. His followers didn't appear to be troubled by any contradictions between his spirituality and the lavish events he hosted and sold to the general public. An international figure, Muktananda spent part of the year in the America and the rest of his time in Europe or India.

Impressed, and gradually deepening my internal relationship with Muktananda, I decided to participate in a weekend retreat hosted by the guru in a Santa Monica ashram, where he was residing for an extended visit. Between the carrots, my devotion to a guru, daily meditation and visits to the ashram, my husband concluded I really *had* gone off the deep end! However, he was glad that both my mental and emotional health seemed to be improving, and he eventually agreed to support my desire to meet Muktananda in person.

I was quite nervous and had no idea what to expect. All his ashrams looked so beautiful in the videos I had seen. Incense, flowers and chanting filled the halls. Dressed in brightly colored saris, the ashram staff and devotees were able to explore meditation caves and serene gardens and attend events in a hall large enough to accommodate 1,000 people. Of course, since chanting and doing yoga increased the appetite, each ashram boasted a wonderful café and dining hall. Muktananda frequently commented that food is digested better if people chant or pray while preparing the food, and I decided that he was right because the cuisine tasted divine to me!

During the retreat's initiation rite, the guru went from person to person, touching them on the head with a peacock feather. Starting on the opposite side of the room from where I was seated, Muktananda spent three sessions over the course of twenty-four hours to complete the initiation process. Tension filled the room as attendees anticipated what would happen. Indeed, strange manifestations often occurred when his feather touched people: some started crowing like roosters, while others shrieked wildly or gyrated around in strange movements. This did not fulfill my expectations for a serene retreat, but seemed rather like a trip to the zoo!

During our first break, I asked someone for an explanation of the strange reactions, and was told that the sounds and movements were the manifestation of krias (bursts of energy). Krias, she further noted, unblock one's kundalini energy, which originates from the base of the spine. When a guru spiritually activates and awakens one's kundalini energy, it starts to move upward, thus causing the krias's energy boost. According to Hindu teachings, when refined and channeled properly, this energy would bring about one's spiritual transformation.

Still worried, I wondered what would happen to me when the peacock feather eventually made its way over to my head on Sunday morning. As the guru neared my section, he passed me by twice, perhaps because he sensed my resistance. I was still unsettled by all the noises in the room. I surely did not want to crow like a rooster, but neither did I want to miss my opportunity to be initiated by Muktananda's feather. I started to focus on the chanting. Bop, the feather landed on my head, and much to my relief, I maintained my yoga posture and kept my dignity intact.

That afternoon, all 1,000 of the seminar attendees proceeded to receive a blessing from Muktananda. Chanting, in a single line, we moved forward, preparing to meet our guru. Totally self-conscious and self-absorbed, I awkwardly approached and received the blessing. Alas, rather than his acknowledging any special bond between us (I had seen him in my third eye, after all!), Muktananda merely mumbled something in Hindu, gave me a few more peacock taps, and that was it. I drew my Hindu spiritual name out of a box—it read, "Goddess of the Blue Light". That part seemed appropriate, but the rest of the experience left me vaguely disappointed. My first and only retreat with Muktananda felt far less profound than my initiation at home in Oakland. Later that year, I paid the guru another brief visit, but those were the only two times I saw him in person. The visits both disappointed and confused me.

In my special room at home, however, the image of Muktananda continued to appear to me in my dreams and meditations for the next two years. He would visit and instruct me there while I meditated, showing me how to concentrate on regions of my body that needed healing.

Between my internal meditations and the regime I was following with my doctor, my energy and monthly periods returned. Attributing my healing to my guru, I developed a deep spiritual love for Muktananda. He represented an important spiritual stepping stone in my life during those years, as he drew me out of my spiritual isolation and reawakened my desire to seek God. The spiritual ice and bitterness of my heart started to melt; since Muktananda's religious background didn't remind me of my old Catholic guilt, I could listen to him talk about God without reacting. A picture of Christ graced each of his ashrams, hanging alongside his lineage of gurus and other Hindu saints. Muktananda's vision of Paradise, and his Hindu version of Heaven, contained traces and shadows of the true Light I was to discover later. For the first time since I left the Catholic Church, I felt comfortable in a religious setting again.

Chapter 6

Spiritual Healer and Channel

After two years of specialized medical treatment and spiritual healing, the internal visitations from Muktananda stopped. Inspired and hopeful, I continued to meditate, chant and pray using the techniques I had learned. While seeking healing for my bodily ailments, I had awakened my longings for a fulfilling spiritual life. I began to realize that my spirit and body were connected, and that I had a deep desire as well to help others to heal on both levels. My desire to help others heal became the subject of my inner ponderings and in one of my meditations, I saw myself with my hands-on others. Since I had left college, I had been searching for my calling. I was envious of those who knew what they wanted to do with their lives. Could this be my true vocation?

I had been receiving massages for years. Why not learn to give them to others as well? Taking to massage like a duck to water, I discovered I had a talent for intuitively knowing exactly where to place my hands-on people. Within a matter of months, while still completing my studies, I developed a booming massage practice. As I incorporated my meditation skills into my massage sessions, my meditation room became my healing arts studio. I studied cranial work, polarity, acupressure and other disciplines. With the addition and integration of each new technique, I felt my healing abilities deepen. I even started to receive messages for my clients when I laid my hands on them. Becky was right – I did have a talent as a spiritual healer.

Several years had passed and I had lost touch with Becky. She had moved suddenly, leaving no forwarding address or phone number. I was perplexed. There were times when I longed to have a session with her guides, especially after my guru's visitations ceased. I missed the intimacy and spiritually expansive nature of her sessions and my guru's visitations. I started searching for a replacement, looking for the next movement. Once again, my best friend Nancy found a new frontier for me to explore when she introduced me to the Michael Teachings and Michael.

In a group channeling experience, Michael was introduced to us as an entity of more than 1,000 souls that spoke as one voice, but only through chosen individuals on the physical plane. This ancient teaching, we were told in our subsequent sessions, could instruct us about our past lives, the difference between younger and older souls, higher planes, essence twins (soul mates) and much more. Fascinated, I attended as many channeling sessions as I could afford. The Michael Teachings dovetailed nicely with my Hindu spiritual practice and seemed to enhance it.

I studied and memorized the Michael Teachings's intricate system of personal analysis. I learned how to figure out the "soul age" of someone and could talk with others about how their unique combination of personality traits affected their personal growth and their relationships. Much like astrology, the Michael Teachings purported to help people know themselves and believe in their destinies. After a year of study, I requested permission during a private session with our elder channel to be granted the privilege of becoming a channel for Michael, and according to the elder, Michael agreed.

A group of other students and channels gathered for my debut. Relaxing first into a meditative state, I was subsequently overwhelmed by a sudden, intense surge of energy. In an intoxicating, trance-like yet conscious state, I felt the presence of the entity, Michael, and I felt their collective thoughts. For an hour, their words became my words, until they left me and I came back to earthly reality, feeling exhausted and thrilled. With truly little understanding of the nature of this spiritual realm, I thus began my career as a Michael Channel.

As a budding channel, I envisioned myself as a conduit through which healing energies and thoughts from higher planes and enlightened beings flowed. Nothing seemed strange anymore; my aunt's tea leaf and card readings, my experiences with Becky and her guides and the visitations of Muktananda all seemed to lead to my work with Michael. I felt quite at home in my new role as psychic healer and channel.

I did know enough, however, to have concerns about demonic energies and negative forces, and Michael assured us that the techniques taught to us during our sessions protected us and guaranteed us interaction with only positive spiritual activity. Michael also promised me that I was discerning enough to recognize the difference between good and evil, and I believed what I was told. I also felt proud of my accomplishments. Following the directions we were given, and teaching them to others, I felt I had moved up the enlightenment ladder of success. It never occurred to me that my rapid assent might have a dark side.

As always, I based my beliefs on my feelings and emotions. During our sessions, I experienced sensations that felt extraordinary, intense and real. Previously, I had trusted Becky and my guru during his visitations, and I still craved the intimacy I felt with my guides when I entered into a meditative trance state. In turn, I wanted to share this spiritual plane with my clients. Over time, my massage work became more meditative and less physical. Listening to beautiful music, practicing yogic breathing and going into semi-hypnotic trances transported my clients and me into another world, one where I believed we were finding healing and transformation of soul and body.

Convinced that I was experiencing personal transformation and transcendence, I began to believe that with the help of my guides and my meditations, I could transform my negative ego and evolve to a higher state of being, both in this life and the next. I believed that achieving these higher states of being would eventually allow me and others to leave our earthly lives and transcend to even higher states of being that did not require a body. I could become a guide there, so my thinking went, living as they did, and helping others to acquire higher states of being.

Because of my abilities to enter the spiritual realm, people would sometimes ask me to clear their houses of ghosts and negative entities and energies. Several of us might gather in a house where the inhabitants believed that haunted spirits or bad energy dwelled. We would enter into a trancelike channeling state to learn about the history of the house and its otherworldly, unwelcome guests. If past violence or tragedy had marked the houses, we were able to perceive the souls, still trapped between the planes of existence. We would let them speak "through" us, telling their stories. Often, their stories and the lives of the current owners of the house seemed connected in some way. In our work, we endeavored to encourage the trapped souls to move on, so that the owners of the house could be at peace. I felt excited by these encounters, almost as if I were part of a Hollywood movie plot.

Being a channel and a healer opened up a whole new world to me, one where I felt safe, successful and intimately connected with others. I had finally found my niche. When I failed in my goals to become a French teacher and I dropped out of college, it had been a real blow. I had always been a good student who wanted to learn and succeed, and I resented what had happened to me in college. As a child, I used to gather younger children together and teach them. From a very early age, I had wanted to become a teacher, and I idolized some of my teachers in grade school. Our school principal was a compassionate, but tough, young nun, and an excellent instructor. A few times when I broke the rules, my punishment was to be with her after school. At first I was terrified, but her manner was so calm and clear that I accepted my punishment almost eagerly. She would ask me to write out some sort of repentant statement 300 times while she chaperoned me; I groaned, of course, but I secretly loved being in her presence and I learned a great deal during my quiet time with her. My secret hope was that when I grew up, I would be like her.

My high school French teacher, Mrs. Gavin, was dynamic, traditional, strict and structured. She knew how to bring out the best in her students. I loved her and looked forward to each of her classes. With her encouragement, I chose French as my major in college, hoping to follow her example. My English teacher, Mr. Farley, encouraged me to write and I became the editor of our high school paper. Both he and my piano teacher were revolutionary and progressive, and they encouraged me to think for myself. My first yoga teacher, Mara Diamond, left a positive impression on me as well.

I truly desired to influence others the way my teachers had influenced me. Starting with EST, I had been able to pursue an educational career again, but in a non-traditional manner. Indeed, the new things I was learning seemed so much more important to me than what I could have learned in college. The opportunity to become a teacher finally occurred when several of my channeling peers encouraged me to begin teaching others to channel. Thrilled, I struggled through my first year with little mentoring or instruction. Even though I was winging it, I loved it! I offered my classes for a reduced price, inviting my students to have patience with me and make each class a learning experience. Starting from square one, I put together a curriculum over the course of several years and began creating a handbook. As a channel and teacher, I always wanted to encourage healing, intimacy and learning. My students and I experienced a deep form of bonding, quite similar to my experiences with my guru and Becky. Many of my students became my close friends as we shared spurts of creativity and spiritual insights together. Whenever I learned something new, I'd tell my students about it, and together, we felt we were discovering hidden mysteries of the universe.

I was finally *someone*. My clients loved me. I felt special and needed. I even secretly believed that my soul had matured and become so enlightened that I had risen above earthly suffering. Sometimes I felt as if I were walking three feet above the ground. When troubled, I would meditate or talk with my guides. With the next level of spiritual development knocking at my door, I fully expected to be a major player in the New Age. Spiritualism, I believed, would surpass religion and render it obsolete.

Chapter 7

Unexpected Events

Out of the blue one afternoon, Becky called. I was nearly 30 years old and hadn't heard from her for several years. "Where have you been? Where are you living now? Why did you move?" The questions tumbled out of me. She told me that she had moved to Los Angeles, was married and had a baby.

"How are you?" she asked in turn. I recounted my struggles and successes, and attributed them to her guidance and to my experiences with Muktananda. I went on to tell her about the Michael movement and my work as a psychic healer and teacher. I expected her to react with enthusiasm, but on the other end of the phone, she was silent. "Are you still there, Becky?" I asked. "Yes, Polly, I am, but I have something to share with you", she ventured. "Okay, what is it?" I asked, completely unprepared for what was coming next.

"I have become a Christian," Becky stated in a soft voice.

Now I was the one to remain silent. Hearing her words, I felt as if the floor had dropped out from under my feet.

"How did that happen"? I asked, scarcely believing my ears. She began to tell me about her conversion and I tried to absorb the story, but I was in a state of shock. She had "accepted Christ" and joined a fundamentalist Protestant church with her new husband.

"How could you give up everything I now treasure? How could you do such a thing?" I implored. Apparently, my Catholic wounds and guilt still lingered as a bitter taste in my mouth. I surprised even myself with my instant, vehement reaction.

I had never felt at ease with Evangelical Christianity. The more deeply I became involved with channeling and the *New Age,* the more angry and disturbed I would feel when listening to born again Christians. When Becky began to speak about her love for Jesus, and how channeling was of the devil, I ended the conversation, unable to bear what she was saying any further. How could she believe these things? She was my role model and one of the catalysts for my new life! What had happened to her?

A few months later, Becky called again. Calmer this time, and glad that she had worked up the courage to call me, I accepted Becky's invitation to visit her in her new home in Los Angeles. Becky still hoped we could be friends. We had both enjoyed each other's company in the past, so perhaps the best way for her to share her story with me would be over a long weekend? I was intrigued and grateful for the opportunity to make amends. I was also still troubled, and by this time curious, about why she chose to be a Christian.

During our weekend together, Becky did her best to explain to me how she loved Jesus and how she had "accepted Him as her Savior." Much to my dismay, I began to feel ill again as she started sharing her experiences. Inside I was asking, "Why do born again Christians sound the same? Why does 'Accepting Jesus as my Savior' make me want to throw up?" I could barely listen. Then she started to talk about her former guides. "They were demonic, sourced in Satan, you know!"

I went over my edge again. "Becky, please stop." I implored. "I cannot bear to hear any more. I simply cannot believe that what helped me to heal was sourced in Satan. I don't agree with you and can't accept what you're saying. Let's just be friends and let the rest go." Our weekend ended on a pleasant but sad note. I just couldn't warm up to Fundamentalist Christianity. Clearly, we were living in different worlds. My weekend visit was the last time we saw each other, but her conversion and words haunted me. I couldn't understand what she had done and why.

The next unexpected event that occurred in my late 20s was the death of my guru in India. When Muktananda passed away, a part of me died with him, and in deep sorrow, I cried for days. A crushing loneliness descended upon me. What was I going to do? Who would I turn to for solace? Who would be with me in my sacred, interior spaces? Unlike my guides, Muktananda was a person. Nonetheless, it had not crossed my mind that he would someday die and I would be left to live in the void created by his departure.

Soon after my guru died, I decided to experiment with an unusual form of therapy, drug-induced shamanic journeys. I had avoided drugs when I was younger — they scared me. Growing up when the use of LSD and other hallucinatory drugs were widely used by young people for recreational purposes, I remembered well the stories of teens that went over the edge during their *trips* and committed suicide. Despite my fears, my desire to delve deeper into the inner recesses of my soul eventually outweighed my fears; after all, shamanic journeys induced by herbs and plants had been used by native cultures for centuries for spiritual purposes.

Carlos Castenada's popular books described such journeys and after reading them, I could see the potential for spiritual transformation offered through this path, and thought I could somehow find the solace I was seeking since the passing of my guru. Through contacts in several of my communities, I found what I was looking for. I interviewed to become a participant with a group that was researching the therapeutic value of supervised, drug-induced journeying and was accepted into their program. Each journey was supervised to help ensure that if any difficulties arose, someone with experience would be there to support the participants safely through their journey.

We referred to the substances we were taking as medicine, because our purpose in using these substances was to heal aspects of our psyche. I was instructed to start keeping a journal and I began to extensively prepare. I felt more secure knowing my support person would be on standby if help were needed. Before beginning, we spoke about our goals for the journey and what we wanted to discover about ourselves. Then it was down the hatch with the medicine! I was on my way. We wore eye pads and listened to beautiful music throughout the "journey," the crescendos and harmonies propelling us forward into our inner worlds.

My first journey lasted eight hours. As it unfolded, images flashed before me, starting from what I perceived to be the beginning of time. I saw intricate and sublime connections between all peoples; after several hours of feeling utter awe and amazement, I asked internally, "What makes all this possible?" Then in big neon rainbow colors, flashing repeatedly over and over again, I saw the word "GOD"! What can I say? God works in mysterious ways and has a sense of humor, and there in my drug-induced state, I believe He reached out to me. Who else could have orchestrated such beauty and all of life? Of course, God is the source of all things! Flashing neon lights and all, I experienced a profound healing that day, one that permanently altered my relationship with God. My desire to know and be with God rekindled; I never again doubted that He reigned as the Supreme Being and Source of all good things. My first supervised shamanic journey deeply touched my spirit, and I decided to continue to take supervised journeys on a monthly basis.

During one of my journeys, I conceived the idea of starting a foundation. Even the name of it came to me - "The Foundation for Inner Guidance and Light." Picturing a lotus flower opening with stars springing from its heart, I created a logo for my business and a cover for the first book, *Channeling, a Bridge to Transcendence*, that I had begun to write. Other journeys I participated in deepened my love and sense of connection with God. I remember a journey of 24 hours: I was lying with my hands facing up and outward for hours, receiving love from God. As a flower opens in the warmth of the sun, I was opening to His love warming my soul; every fiber of my being then loved Him in return. Not since I was a child had I experienced such intense love for and with God.

The comfort of my journeys helped me as I faced the pain of my marriage unraveling. What I could not see as time passed, even with my vaunted psychic abilities, was that my marriage had been in trouble for many years; we were both in a state of hope and denial about our predicament. Peter and I had grown apart. Our values and goals had gradually changed, but neither of us wanted to admit that our fundamental problems were not resolving themselves, even as we continued participating in a multitude of seminars and workshops to help strengthen our marriage.

We had learned to better respect and communicate with each other, but I wasn't able to step out of recurring and unhealthy patterns of interaction with him. My spiritual yearnings drove me; Peter was much more down to earth than I. We could set goals and work well together, but we functioned better as friends than lovers, which eventually lead to irreconcilable differences from my perspective.

Sitting alone in my car one day, I sobbed. What was my life and marriage really about? I was scared of the idea of being on my own but I was miserably unhappy. Reaching inside for courage to utter the words I had dreaded saying for years, I asked for a divorce. I could not see how a separation would work, even though Peter pleaded for this move first. I moved out of our house in three weeks, and in six months filed for and completed our divorce. Although not caught completely by surprise, for folks had known for some time that we were struggling, our parents and many of our friends were devastated.

Chapter 8

Chance Meetings

After our marriage disintegrated, I felt as if I had entered into an altered reality – one that felt foreign and strange to me. For better and for worse, I had spent thirteen years of my life with my husband. Confused and disoriented, I increased my visits to the ashram until it became my sanctuary. Living with several other EST friends provided me with a temporary spot to land, but I lacked clear direction. Now that I had left my unhappy marriage, where was I going to find the internal happiness I so desperately craved?

During those first few months, I spent quite a bit of time with my channeling friends. One memorable evening, I remarked to my friends that my impending divorce had given me the opportunity to find a new legal name. A return to my maiden name, Paula Angela Sivori, seemed awkward, since I felt much more at ease with my childhood nickname, Polly.

My friends suggested I choose a new last name that was more akin to my true personality and soul, one that I could use professionally and legally. Oddly enough, although I'd left my Catholicism behind, we all gravitated towards the name, "Polly St. Something". With much humor, we experimented with at least thirty of these Polly names before I chose Polly St. John. I had always loved the Gospel according to St. John and this felt right. Needless to say, my parents and aunt weren't as thrilled with my proposed name change. They couldn't imagine why I wouldn't use my maiden name once again. I tried to explain to them that I couldn't relate to it, but in the end, they threw their hands up in the air, frustrated and hurt. I apologized and asked them to bear with me.

In December, 1982, four months after leaving Peter, I decided to make a pilgrimage to India in an attempt to reconcile my past and discover my future. Unlike my connection with Muktananda, I felt no spiritual attraction to his successor, a woman, and I wanted to resolve that confusion as well. Initially, I planned to fly directly to India, but when I discovered that it was a 36-hour flight across the Pacific Ocean to Bombay, I looked at other options. I wasn't that zealous of a disciple! My travel agent then said the magic words, "Why not fly around the world?" He mentioned stopovers in Geneva, Florence and then, best of all, *Paris*. My heart leapt! I was sold. I purchased a one-way, round-the-world ticket, heading east, for only $1,500.00. My crushed dreams of being a French teacher as a young college student revived the moment the thought of traveling to Paris became a reality.

My family's journey to America in search of a better life lived in me. They had risked everything to leave behind the abject poverty they had endured in Italy. I was willing to take the same risks to enrich my impoverished spirit. I sensed that my soul's very existence depended upon my upcoming adventure. I knew that if I could just get on the plane and keep going, that my life would change.

With the reluctant support of my parents, I boarded a plane in San Francisco in the middle of January, 1983, headed for Europe. My parents were worried. They had witnessed my marital breakdown and ensuing unhappiness. They knew I needed to do something. As usual, I chose rather unconventional means to achieve my goals. My dad understood my motivations, however, remembering his rail-riding adventures as a hobo at the age of 16. Well, if my dad was a risk taker, so was I! I didn't tell them that I only had $450 set aside for the entire trip. My initial destinations included Switzerland, Italy, Paris, India, Bangkok, Hong Kong and Maui. I had personal connections in Europe and India, but the rest of my journey was unknown. I decided to keep a journal of my adventure.

"I want to deepen my relationship with the essence in myself that is God," I wrote in one of my first entries. *"I have a longing to be connected and*

complete that is difficult to put into words. My hope is that I can reach this experience fully through Baba (the familiar name given to Muktananda) *by going to India. It is India or bust! I will find myself in India. Regarding healing and channeling: I want to serve and bring 'Michael' and other masters to their students. I want to make a difference in their lives and mine. I intend to have good solid relationships and connections with people. I want my French to blossom."*

Even before I landed in Geneva, my first destination, the blessings of my journey started to unfold. On the plane between London and Switzerland, I met a fascinating, eloquent man who was a radio journalist in Sri Lanka. We developed a friendship within a few hours. Intrigued with my profession and adventure, he urged me to go to Sri Lanka rather than Bangkok, cautioning me that single women were unsafe in Bangkok. He gave me his phone number and address just before we landed in Geneva. "When you arrive in Sri Lanka, give me a call and I'll help you."

I arrived in Switzerland three days before my baggage. I was staying with two women who were friends of a friend, and they were kind enough to lend me some of their clothing until my luggage arrived. After sleeping fifteen hours straight, I awoke to a winter wonderland. I fell in love with the cobblestone streets, the quaint houses and chalets, the food, the trains, the museums and the Swiss supermarkets! My new friends helped me to adjust and explore. The *piece de resistance* of my first week in Europe occurred when I traveled around Lake Geneva to go skiing and stay with one of my friend's aunts in Lucerne. An elderly, petite Swiss woman, she lived in a picturesque Swiss chalet. As I sat drinking hot chocolate, watching snow slide down her windowpane, my mind went back to Shirley Temple playing the part of Heidi. As a child, I watched all of the Shirley Temple movies and now I felt like Heidi, hot chocolate and all! In my mountain chalet, this aunt of my friend could have been my Swiss grandmother.

Returning to family roots of a different kind, I spent my second week with my Italian cousins in northern Italy. As the first American family member to return to my father's homeland, I received a warm welcome. I will never forget my sixty-year old cousin running down the train tracks shouting, "Paola! Paola!" (Italian for Paula) tears of joy streaming down her face as she welcomed me. In a whirlwind of questions concerning my family and what kind of food I preferred, we drove to their home in Riva Trigoso, a village on the Italian Mediterranean. My cousins were so kind and generous to me that I felt as if I were a member of the Royal Family.

I loved Italy and being with my Italian family. After a few days, we went to visit my dad's breathtakingly beautiful natal village, Velva, in the foothills about a 45-minute drive away. We met an old woman who remembered my dad, my grandmother and my aunts, and she shared some stories with me about my family and father. From there, we drove to Genoa, Pizza, Florence and parts of the Italian Mediterranean. My relatives would not let me pay for anything and showered me with gifts. When the day of our parting arrived, we were all in tears.

I then boarded an overnight train to Paris, where I had planned to stay for two weeks with a Parisian family friends thought I should visit. I was warmly welcomed into their Paris flat by Sam (the father), Claire (the mother), Lara (their daughter) and Noah (their son). We seemed to connect quickly and easily as we shared our stories. Claire's gripping tale brought me to tears. I soon realized why our mutual friend had insisted that I look them up when I arrived in Paris.

A hidden child during World War II, Claire had lost her father, and all of her father's family, when they were deported to the death camp at Auschwitz. Claire and her mother were not able to escape from France, but her mother was able to hide Claire with a Catholic woman who resided about thirty miles outside of Paris. Her only contact with her mother for several years during the war was a monthly visit to the subway station. She would gaze at her mother across the subway tracks. They could do nothing to indicate they knew each other or their lives would have been in danger.

Prior to my arrival, Claire had been diagnosed with melanoma cancer in her right eye. Usually people with this form of cancer live only six months to one year. She had already made it through the first six months after the diagnosis when I met her. Claire woke up each morning with anxiety and excruciating pain in her right eye which persisted throughout the day.

In spite of, and perhaps because of her suffering, Claire had a wisdom that was no-nonsense, practical and to the point. Her experiences past and present impelled her to see and embrace reality, in

42

contrast to my persistent escapism. For Claire, connection with other people and creating a sense of family were preeminent goals. What she valued most was unconditional love and reliability. Because her life had been spared during the war, Claire cared about life and other people with a tenacity that went beyond words, and she fiercely fought injustice. Her goal of peaceful co-existence on a personal and global level, madeClaire was one of the most unselfish people I had ever met. While fighting for her own survival, she had also become grateful for the gift of each day.

Claire's husband, Sam, was equally inspiring. Sam began and ended each day with a smile. Sam's quiet wisdom and humility complemented Claire's intensity. He was totally devoted to Claire and his children. I admired them both, and quickly became a member of their family. I cooked and shopped for them, joined them when they went skiing in the Italian Alps and when they journeyed to the beaches of the Normandy Coast.

Noah gave me his room so I could work with Claire, and eventually others, in a private space. Each day I would spend several hours allowing healing energy to fl ow through my hands to Claire. After each session, the pain in her eye decreased and her anxiety lessened. I also offered classes twice a week on the Michael Teaching for my new family and friends. In turn, Claire supported me as I reevaluated my life.

Claire slowly improved. Grateful for my help, she shared her healing breakthroughs with her friends, who quickly called me to schedule sessions. Two weeks turned into almost two months, as I decided to stay longer in France than originally planned. I had so much work to do and I hadn't even seen Paris yet! My childhood yearning to be a French teacher reawakened and my love of the French language blossomed. I was channeling, teaching others about Michael and helping others to heal, all while speaking in French. I was finally a French teacher in my own unique way.

Here are a few entries from my journal. "*Everything is moving very fast and beyond what I thought could be possible. I am seeing my power and it comes from love. I have a tremendous capacity to love and when I come from love, I am powerful.*" Michael would speak to me, "*We want to acknowledge you for your growth and love. Your channeling and clarity about us have all been beyond our greatest hopes for you and others. We love working with you.*"

When I could, I did take excursions to Versailles, Chartres and the French countryside. Additionally, thanks to Claire and her friends, I earned the money I needed to fund the rest of my trip. During our time together, I sorted out fundamental problems I had experienced in my relationships with men, starting with my dad. I had a nasty habit of holding onto resentments against others, particularly with my father and men in general. This became our routine every day: I worked with Claire in my healing capacity for several hours a day, and then, in turn, she spoke with me about my life and struggles. From her, I learned that I was quite egocentric and often lived in my own internal world, separated from others. I would selfishly wait for others to act and do things for me that I thought I needed from them, but only rarely did I communicate to others what I wanted or needed from them, assuming that they should know. To complete the cycle of bitterness, I would then blame them when they did not act on my assumptions and expectations.

Claire had noticed that while I was staying with her, I was upset and hurt that my dad had not written me. My mother sent me letters of course, but my dad would only sign his name. Uncomfortable with writing because of his limited education, my dad left the written communications to my mom.

Claire helped me begin to see how I had judged, blamed and separated myself from my dad as a teenager. Lonely and angry, I went looking for my dad in other men. Obviously, these other men could not fill the shoes of my father, so I judged, blamed and separated myself from them as well! No wonder my relationships with men were not working. She suggested that perhaps I could take some responsibility for what I wanted and needed from my dad. I started writing him short postcards every other day to tell him how much I missed and loved him. Claire suggested that I keep them simple. I realized that I needed to make an effort to communicate with my dad, rather than focus on what he was not doing for me.

After two months of working with Claire almost daily, she was experiencing only occasional pain. For my part, I began to release some of my bitterness towards my loved ones. What an extraordinary interval of time it had been for both of us. It was now mid-April and I was ready, but quite anxious, about my departure for India.

Chapter 9

India

As my plane approached the Bombay runway, I recalled the stories my ashram friends told about getting off the plane in India and being surrounded and overwhelmed by beggars. I knew I would be stretching my comfort levels by entering into truly foreign territory. How would I react to the poverty in India, and would I get sick? I had arranged for a friend to meet me in Bombay, but I was a month and a half late. Although I had sent Jodi a letter, I had no idea if she had received it. Much to my relief, there were not hundreds of beggars to greet me when I arrived, just my friend. She quickly escorted me to a cab and we were on our way to Bombay.

I arrived in the middle of India's hottest season. The British apparently would go north to Kashmir to escape the stifling 120-degree heat and I quickly understood why. Thankfully, the breezes from the Indian Ocean, reminding me of the winds of San Francisco Bay, took the edge off the harshness of my first day as we walked and toured the seaside part of the city. My friend introduced me to street shopping and chai, Indian tea with lots of caffeine, sugar and milk. I felt as if I had been plugged into a light socket, glowing for hours, after my first, and only, cup of chai.

After our tour of Bombay, we hailed a cab - I was finally off to the ashram to fulfill my spiritual dreams. We were only a long cab ride away from my hoped-for spiritual paradise, but what a cab drive! The cab drivers in India appeared to be playing chicken with the oncoming traffic, all the while honking their horns at everything in sight. The cabbie's noise, multiplied many times over by the number of drivers on the road, made the ride to the ashram unforgettable. Between the chai and the cab ride, I was ready for peace and quiet. As we entered the ashram, the harshness of India disappeared, eclipsed by the exquisitely beautiful surrounding gardens. Although abject poverty was right outside the door of the ashram, the inside was a seeming paradise.

We checked in and were escorted to our dorm room. Expecting a private room and perhaps a way to escape the heat, we were ushered into a large room with at least twenty other women - no fans, no privacy and primitive bathrooms. The shower consisted of a bucket or two of cold water poured over one's head and the bathrooms required squatting. Clearly, I hadn't checked into a four-star hotel in India. After dinner, we spent some time in the primary meditation hall until I went to bed, exhausted. Too hot and uncomfortable to sleep, I spent a fitful night up on the roof in search of cooler temperatures, sharing the space with bugs and a cacophony of animals who howled, groaned, mooed, crowed and chattered until the wee hours of the morning.

I woke from a fitful sleep to a beautiful sunrise and joined the morning meditation. Already wondering how I would adjust to three weeks of life in the ashram, I spoke with Jodi at breakfast, who announced that she planned to leave in two days! She had waited for me for one month and was ready to go visit other friends and gurus. Did I want to stay in the ashram or go with her?

I spent my day visiting the meditation halls, walking the gardens and praying at the grave of my guru. For years, I had thought that when I finally entered the ashram in India, my search for internal peace and spiritual happiness would be over. Now I realized that once again, my ideals and reality had clashed.

Far from being a peaceful haven, India was noisy and impoverished. Night and day, animals and birds added their squawking to the sounds of honking horns, trains and mechanical noises. Cows, chickens and people lived on the streets anywhere and everywhere. Gahneshpuri, the city of the ashram, sheltered me from this somewhat, since it boasted a measure of Western comforts due to all the international devotees who frequented the ashram. The India of 1983 also lacked much of the technology I'd grown accustomed to in my daily life. Their phones resembled the phones we used in America during the 1920s and '30s and frequently didn't work. Taxis and small rickshaws, which were the most common and inexpensive form of transportation, provided employment for the impoverished local residents. On one occasion when I was riding in a motorized rickshaw, it broke down and the driver fixed it with chewing gum! Errands, like a simple run to the post office or bank, could take all day; it took three hours, sitting at five different desks with twenty different clerks, to get my travelers checks cashed!

At the ashram, I hadn't expected to find the elitism and the cliques that existed there. Rather than the spiritually uplifting atmosphere I had hoped to find, many pilgrims seemed discontented, uneasy and troubled. Many could not leave because they had run out of money while waiting and hoping for their lives to change. I never did manage to meet my guru's successor, who was struggling with back problems. My decision to leave the ashram with my friend was easier to make than I had anticipated.

Jodi and I took an overnight train to New Delhi. Stepping off the train with my body in the beginning throes of dysentery, I was overwhelmed by another wave of culture shock. The streets were filthy and dusty and the polluted air smelled rancid. On the street, I saw dying people lying by the roadside. Getting into a cab with my friend, I wept with shock and homesickness.

I am not sure how I would have survived my first week in India without my friend's companionship. In the suburbs of New Delhi, Jodi had arranged for us to stay with her friends, a minister and his wife, in their lovely home. Stressed and sick, I collapsed in their guest bedroom for the next forty-eight hours. I better understood now the accounts I had heard of Westerners suffering nervous breakdowns in India. Slowly, I began to adjust to my new environment and venture out of the house.

After a week, Jodi decided to go north to Kashmir in search of another well-known guru, but before she left, we visited an Indian family she had befriended to share a meal. They treated us as honored guests and after we left, Jodi told me they had probably spent a month's worth of their wages to provide us with that simple meal. With Claire, I had learned the value of cherishing those you love; in India, I learned to be more grateful and simple. In America, sometimes our material wealth stands in stark contrast to our spiritual impoverishment. Many of the Indians I met were poor, yet so gracious and hospitable, offering the best that they had to offer. In contrast, I had never gone without anything myself, in order to give to others. India had a beauty not readily apparent at first, that which resided in the expansive and hospitable hearts and souls of her people.

After ten days in India, I felt better prepared to journey alone. On the day of my departure, I took the plane, train, bus and taxi, returning safely to the ashram without a hitch! I was hoping that my second sojourn at the ashram would be more fulfilling. My first night back, however, was one of the worst of my life. Feeling crazy from the unbearable heat, I wrote: *"Baba, I am scared and feel awful. I know that I am not the fear and worries I feel, but I am not at peace. Baba, help me and guide me. I am going to get through this night and somehow enjoy my stay here."* Venturing off the roof, where I'd been lying to escape the oppressive atmosphere below, I started conversing with a woman sitting on the stairs who was reading by a dim light. Much to my relief, she said, "Oh, you're not going crazy, it's this place! I 've been trying to leave for weeks!" Shree (her spiritual name) had already paid for a several month stay and the ashram wouldn't refund anyone's money once they had registered. Many Americans were apparently stranded because they could not afford to leave, and were waiting for family and friends to wire money to them. Shree also wanted to leave but was too frightened to travel alone in India.

We made a plan. We were going to escape! We devised an itinerary for our final twelve days which included Nasik, the home city of our deceased guru, so that we might meet one of Muktananda's disciples, Swami Prokasananda. Shree had heard from others that this disciple was a good man. To arrive at our destination, we took a five-hour bus ride through rural India. We passed through countless small villages with women in colorful saris carrying water, wood and pots on their heads, and people living in grass huts who waved as we went by. In Nasik, a large city, we managed to find our swami's humble abode. Prokasananda lived in a building that was part medical clinic, part ashram, owned and operated by a young Indian doctor and his wife.

One floor of their building was given to the guru for his living quarters, reception and meditation area, one floor was for guests and the first floor was for the clinic where they served the poor.

The hospitality and caring we received in Nasik were what Shree and I had hoped to find at Muktananda's ashram. We shared a room, cooled by a fan, and we all gathered for prayers and food twice daily. I was continually struck by the contrast between Muktananda's ashram and the humble clinic/ashram of Swami Prokasananda. What a humble but intimate welcome we were given. Rather than a massive meditation hall, he had one designated meditation room. Instead of sitting on a velvet throne with beautiful surroundings, as Muktananda had done, he reclined on a plastic lounge chair. Instead of an elaborate donation box, he kept a rubber tub at his feet where local residents deposited fresh fruit. Instead of being surrounded by hundreds of people, we sat with a handful of other devotees.

The Swami spoke with us about our hopes for our journey. As I reflected that evening on the intimate conversation we had shared with him, I recalled how disappointed I had felt after each of my pilgrimages to see Muktananda in person. In spite of my inner relationship with Baba, I lacked any personal relationship with him, and felt self-conscious and awkward at the gatherings in Santa Monica when he was present.

The next morning our humble guru surprised us by serving us breakfast! I wrote, *"I know that Swami-gi is not wealthy, but what he has, he shares. I was in tears after he treated us to a wonderful Indian breakfast. I have developed an appreciation for the humility of the Indian people. How blessed we have been to be given so much from those that have so little. Swami-gi encouraged us to lick our plate! Apparently licking your plate is a courtesy. Food is too precious to waste, especially food blessed by a guru. I feel God and my Baba have brought me to this little haven in India – it is an answer to my prayers."*

Our host surprised us with our next gift. He had arranged a tour for us of all of the holy places where Muktananda had been, including a visit to the Ganges River. We spent the next several hours touring the Hindu temples where Muktananda had studied, and where he had been initiated as a monk and achieved enlightenment. In one temple, a 95-year-old man who had known Muktananda since childhood gave us a tour of the grounds. Shree and I were delighted and inspired. Our driver then took us to the Ganges River where elephants, oxen and people were gathered on the banks, bathing or washing their clothes. The river shimmered, reflecting a beautiful array of colors from the buildings and temples that lined its shore. By this point in my journey, I was glad I had come.

Our tour included a stop at a marketplace, where I purchased a black beaded necklace from one of the vendors. Suddenly, all the surrounding women started to engage me in conversation. "Where is your husband? Do you have children?" Up until this point of my journey in India, people had hesitated to make eye contact with me or engage me in conversation. Women had apparently been afraid to speak with me and the men looked at me as if I were a loose woman. I discovered that in India, women who were not married or who were traveling alone were considered to be immoral. Unbeknownst to me, my purchase of the black necklace in the marketplace meant that I was married – it was a wedding necklace. People were willing socialize with me now that they no longer viewed me as a prostitute.

By our final evening in Nasik, I had experienced everything that I wished I could have experienced with Muktananda. In a private audience with Swami-gi, he answered several questions that had troubled me, including one pertaining to my health. The next morning, when we tearfully bid farewell to our new friends and swami, both Shree and I felt spiritually satiated. After returning for a one-night stay at Muktananda's ashram, we traveled to the Indian Ocean for five days, where I gratefully enjoyed the sea breezes and a swim. We lodged at the same inn where the film crew of *Gandhi* stayed when they were shooting scenes of Gandhi (played by Ben Kingsley) making salt at the sea. By the end of our ocean retreat, I felt ready to leave India. I had only twenty days left before I would be home, but it seemed like an eternity. I needed courage and strength to finish the last leg of my voyage. India had given me many lessons and gifts; earning them had taken its toll.

During my last days on India's soil, worn out from the daily 120-degree heat and running out of money again, I received a long, handwritten letter, with cash enclosed, from my dad. Tears streamed down my cheeks. All my post cards and letters had touched him deeply — he missed me and expressed his love for me. My father really did care about me. His letter gave me the courage and the means to keep going.

When I arrived at the Bombay airport, ready to begin my journey home, Air Lanka informed me that they had no record of my reservation. When I produced my ticket, the clerks laughed and said I was supposed to have come to the airport three days in advance to confirm my place on their flight. Then they instructed me to sit down. "We can't promise you a place on our plane, but if there are any seats left after everyone checks in, we'll let you know." I sat down and started praying my mantra and waited for three hours, wondering what I would do if the agents denied me a boarding pass.

About ten minutes before the flight's scheduled departure, the clerks waved to me and said, "Hurry up! There's a seat for you. You have to go through customs before you can board the plane." I received the last and quite uncomfortable seat in the back of the plane, but it didn't matter. Via Sri Lanka, I was on my way home.

The day after I arrived in Sri Lanka, I called the Sri Lankan man I had met on my flight to Switzerland. During our several hours of conversation catching up, he asked me about my plans while passing through Sir Lanka. "What do you suggest?" I asked? He apologized that he was not available to show me around personally and pondered how I might best enjoy visiting his island. With no strings attached, he gifted me with a cab and driver to take me around the entire island for a week, and mapped out the entire itinerary, inns and all. He wanted to make sure I would be safe and yet still see what Sri Lanka had to offer – this included an elephant ride! All I could give him in return was an *Ending Hunger* sweatshirt I had brought for him from Paris, and a grateful hug.

This was the extraordinary nature of my entire trip, wherein my needs were provided for in ways I never could have imagined. After Sri Lanka, I spent three days in Hong Kong with a British family I met on the plane when we were all moved up to first class together. Interested in my work and travel stories, they offered me a much-needed air-conditioned room, hot showers and Chinese food in exchange for my healing services. Their home was an apartment that overlooked Hong Kong Bay, which reminded me of both Hawaii and San Francisco.

Three days later, I boarded the plane to Maui, with a six-hour stopover in Japan, for the final leg of my journey home. Exhausted, infected with Indian parasites and troubled by an aching back, I prayed in desperation that during the layover in Japan I could have a massage to ease the pain. From the airport, I took a taxi into the nearest city. Since I didn't speak Japanese, I kept exclaiming "Shiatsu, Shiatsu!" Finally, the driver caught on and dropped me off at a local spa. Two hunch-backed elderly women greeted me and escorted me to their hot pools and cold plunges. No Shiatsu, but I soaked my cares away, just barely making my 8-hour connecting flight to Hawaii.

Chapter 10

Completions

I kissed the ground when I landed in Hawaii. I was grateful to be an American and so very glad to almost be home. Scenes of poverty lingered in the back of my mind as I made my way through the airport. I remembered the scene in Sri Lanka of men and women, some well advanced in years, filling in potholes on a poorly made road. I had been internally complaining about how rough and bumpy the road was up to that point, until we passed the road repair crew. Rocks ranging from small to boulder size were piled along the roadside. The Sri Lankans chipped and hammered away at these rocks to make them smaller. They hammered away, day after day, in 90-degree heat and 100% humidity, without a chair to sit on. Viewing the grinding poverty in Sri Lanka and India had given me a new pair of eyes.

What awaited me in Hawaii? I was finally going to reconnect with my boyfriend, whom I had met at an EST seminar a few months prior to embarking on my journey. We had corresponded during my long trip and both of us were eager to see each other again. We spent the last week of my trip together on Maui. After I caught him up on my adventures, he then filled me in on what he'd been doing, and delivered news that brought me out of the clouds and down to earth with a painful thump. My ten-year old dog Sasha I left in the care of my roommate had disappeared during my long absence. About three weeks prior, he had simply vanished one day.

I was devastated. When Peter and I were newlyweds, a neighbor had found three-month-old Sasha in a garbage can at a local shopping center. When I left my husband, Sasha stayed on with me as my faithful companion and we had been through many ups and downs together. For days after receiving this news, I was grief stricken, mourning not only the loss of my dear dog, but also my former life. While traveling, I had been too distracted and busy to feel these emotions. My dog's disappearance opened the floodgates of my heart, and I was shocked to discover that I was still grieving the death of my marriage and all that had been my prior life.

At one point, crying about my lost dog and failed marriage by the ocean, I realized that returning home to a new beginning frightened me. I was twenty years old when I first married. Now thirty-one, with a boyfriend about eight years older than me, I knew I needed to grow up. If I could begin a journey around the world with only $450 in my pocket, I could earn a living as a single woman in America, Sam assured me. I knew he was right, yet I struggled to find my way the first few months after I returned. America, the Bay Area and my home all seemed foreign to me. It was not my family or my familiar surroundings that had changed – I had changed. Who was I now? What did I want to do with this new me?

When I reached California, I spent hours with my parents, sharing the details of my adventures and my photographs. My parents and my friends were thrilled that I had returned safe and sound. Yet, I seemed to be experiencing reverse culture shock, feeling out of place on my home territory. Thankfully, Sam and other friends pushed me to let go of my losses and move on. Gradually, I regained my equilibrium; my boyfriend and I moved into his apartment in Walnut Creek, I rolled up my sleeves, revived my dormant private practice and went to work.

Sam was involved with a small but highly committed martial arts group, and he encouraged me to take a class with his charismatic teacher, Darryl. As usual, I was open to trying anything new. An air of secrecy surrounded his martial arts master, and Sam wouldn't tell me anything more than, "You have a lot to learn." Nervous and curious, I showed up for the class, which was held in a local recreational park facility. When

I arrived, I noticed several people already sitting on a hardwood floor in a meditative posture. I usually meditated using a pillow, due to my back problems. Among other things, Sam hadn't warned me that we would be sitting on a bare floor. I surveyed the room for something to sit on. Spotting a rice bag in the corner of the room, I moved it into the meditation area and sat on it, pleased at my ability to improvise.

Several of the higher ranked students arrived shortly thereafter and within minutes, they started frantically searching for something. "What is all the fuss about?" I wondered. Finally, an incredibly handsome muscular man walked into the room, looked around and said, "Does anyone know where my rice bag is?" I sheepishly raised my hand and pointed to the bag I was sitting on. "Is this what you're looking for?" I replied. The room suddenly fell quiet and my mortified boyfriend sat rigidly, waiting for the master's response. Darryl started laughing and graciously asked for his rice bag back. It took Sam a week to recover from my blunder, but I was secretly pleased that I had made a connection with Darryl, albeit through an embarrassing mistake. This was the first of many blunders I would commit during my yearlong adventure into the world of martial arts.

I had never met anyone quite like Darryl. He reminded me of the hero of a popular TV show, Kung Fu, whose hero (like Darryl) sported tattooed dragons on the inside of his arms. Darryl had spent numerous years in the East studying with many different masters in pursuit of his calling. What he taught was a blend of Eastern traditions and martial arts. He moved through space like a tiger, every muscle defined, trained and developed. Graceful, witty, but no-nonsense in manner, Darryl constantly reflected our egos back to us through the grueling 4 to 5-hour workout sessions we attended.

It took me three days to recover physically from each weekly class. Every bone and muscle in my body ached due to lactic acid buildup. I would stand in the shower, alternating between hot and cold water, wishing for a different body, one that was not so sensitive to pain. Even as a teenager, it was a struggle for me to complete aerobic workouts. During the two half-marathons I trained for and ran as fundraising events, my body angrily resisted and I paid dearly for each one. My second half-marathon proved to be too hard on my knees and back and I subsequently quit running.

The routines Darryl put us through required a coordination and strength I lacked, so I failed most of the exercises. I moved out of my comfort zone to stay in Darryl's classes even though I was at the bottom of the class. Why? Part of my continued attendance was due to Sam's participation. I wanted to share in a higher spiritual goal and activity with him. Another part of me knew I was in the presence of someone unique and authentic – someone like Claire. I learned a valuable lesson about myself in Darryl's classes. Th ere, I did not impress anyone! I could not get away with faking it. Other than catching a single piece of toilet tissue on a bamboo stick, my biggest accomplishments that year were to learn to laugh at myself more and become more at peace with failure. Although I was clearly not cut out to pursue martial arts long term, the year I spent with Darryl was worth every aching muscle and moment of embarrassment I endured for the sake of humbling my ego.

I would have continued to attend classes with Darryl, but he decided to retire and travel. My boyfriend and I were simultaneously at a crossroads of our own. In spite of our best efforts, we were clearly not suited for a long-term relationship. Inspired by my global trip, Sam decided to go Europe with an open-ended ticket, and we called our relationship off when he left. I took over our apartment and for the first time in my life was truly on my own.

After we parted company, I participated in a few more supervised shamanic journeys. During these journeys, I began to believe that there had to be another way to create deep intimacy and connection with God, but how? In my most recent journey, I distinctly felt there was yet another way that was unknown to me. I tearfully ended my relationship with shamanic journeys. Additionally, I also ceased participating in EST, since the organization was heading in a new direction and I did not feel called to move on with them. Although I continued to meditate, I stopped going to the ashram as well.

The last shred of my former life vanished when my former husband announced that he and my best friend, Nancy, were getting married! Th e news of their engagement was not easy to accept, to say the least! One can only imagine all the emotions that surfaced as a result of their declared union, and it required every ounce of love I had for each of them to overcome my irrational, though understandable, feelings of loss, resentment and betrayal. After six intense months, I was finally able to accept and bless their relationship. I loved them both and above all, wished to stay friends with them. As did my mom, I believed that no hurt was worth the pain of long-term separation or alienation. One by one, doors closed on each significant area of my life. I believed that something new might be on the horizon and I waited for it to take shape.

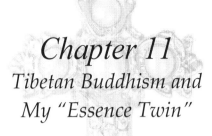

Chapter 11
Tibetan Buddhism and
My "Essence Twin"

One of the hottest topics on the forefront of most of my clients' minds during our channeling sessions was the subject of one's "essence twin." Michael teachers used the term to describe one's soul mate, the person destined to be one's complement. This person was considered to be closest to one's own essence and being. For examples of essence twins, we cited celebrity romantic relationships, as well as identical twins or inseparable friends who had bonded since childhood. We taught that a person could meet one's soul mate in one or more lifetimes, due to reincarnation, and some teachers believed that an essence twin could even be an extraterrestrial being. Clients always wanted to know if *this* lifetime would be the one when they would meet this incomparable person.

Meeting one's essence twin could be a cause for joy or disappointment, depending on the seeker's marital status, set of dysfunctional personality traits or age. Michael warned us that the relationship itself could be quite stormy. Despite the threat and risk, as a single person, I yearned with all my heart to find my essence twin. Still hopelessly romantic, I was waiting for my Prince Charming to come along. In several private sessions with one of my fellow channels, I was told I would soon find him, which intensified my anticipation.

Several months after Sam departed for Europe, a friend suggested that I seek the treatments of a brilliant acupuncturist to help ease both my back pain and the symptoms caused by the persistent Indian parasites plaguing my digestive tract. Not long into my treatment cycle, I began dating my acupuncturist. I felt intensely connected to him and began to hope that he might be my longed-for essence twin. Sure enough, my fellow channels confirmed that I had, indeed, found him. I was in heaven! As a bonus, he was single, handsome, intelligent and spiritual. He didn't think we were essence twins, or even believe in the concept, but I was convinced.

Since my new boyfriend was immersed in Tibetan Buddhism thought and practice, I wasted no time in joining his meditation sessions with his lama and commenced a study of Tibetan Buddhism. Many of its traditions and teachings appealed to me. I appreciated the compassionate aspect of striving not to harm any living thing, and Tibetan spiritual artwork was beautiful and compelling. I loved praying and meditating before the various serene Buddhas portrayed in the artwork, and I began to regret that I hadn't gone to the northern regions of India to visit a few of the Tibetan monasteries during my world tour. Although my new boyfriend followed a different sect, I had a great respect for the Dalai Lama. Besides finding my essence twin, was I also meant to follow the path of Tibetan Buddhism? Was this the spiritual path that would replace the void left by my guru and my shamanic journeys?

After several months, I felt it was time for me to be formally initiated into Tibetan Buddhism, a necessary rite if one is to delve deeper into its teachings. Once initiated, I could then participate in retreats and advance level classes with my boyfriend. I arranged to have his lama come to my house, inviting many friends and clients as well. That evening, the lama gave me a Tibetan spiritual name, "Goddess of the Lotus Flower," which I added to my growing list of spiritual names. Around the same time, my boyfriend moved into his lama's residence, which was also our local Tibetan temple. He moved his acupuncture practice into two rooms in the temple and lived in a third, becoming the personal healer for his lama and our Tibetan community.

Several months after this move, my relationship with my boyfriend began to change; he proposed we take a break. "Let's be friends for a while," he suggested. I agreed, still believing this to be part of the essence twin pattern. Wasn't the relationship supposed to be stormy? I fully expected that after a time we would resolve our issues, for how could I possibly let go of my essence twin, now that I had found him? A few months later, I signed up for a 24-hour retreat – mostly to see him - although we spoke often on the phone. Going into the retreat, my unspoken hope and expectation was that seeing each other again in this spiritual context would bring us closer. However, nothing was further from the truth. My hopes were dashed - we remained more separated than ever. Instead of feeling spiritually satiated and emotionally close to my essence twin, I drove home from the 24-hour event feeling empty and lost. What was I going to do?

In addition to my dwindling hope for a relationship with my essence twin, I was also somewhat disturbed by some of the artwork depicting demonic Buddhas. In both the Hindu and Tibetan traditions, I watched others pray before a demonic Hindu god or a Tibetan Buddha, such as the entity Kali. Perhaps due to my Catholic background, praying in front of, or to, these demonic portrayals unnerved me, and I refused to do so as my inner alarm bells went off at the prospect. For these reasons, my visits to the Tibetan temple became less frequent. Eventually, I stopped going altogether and returned to practicing my own form of meditation at home.

Desperately holding on to a sinking ship, I sought out my trusted sources, my fellow Michael channels. "Do not give up hope", they said. "Connect with him on 'inner planes'." "Inner planes, of course – that is where I can find him," I said with relief. "If I work hard to connect with him on inner planes, he'll come back to me." For months, I focused on connecting with him, aided by my guides. I sincerely believed we were connecting on a spiritual level and continued to seek the counsel of my channeling friends and astrologers to ensure that I would achieve the desired result. They validated and reinforced my hopes and desires. "You'll be reunited with him soon," they said. "You are destined to be together. You are on the right track."

Over time, however, I began to question what I was doing and awaken from my self-created delusion. It was as if I were in a psychic soap opera. I gradually realized that I had been living in a world based on fantasy. I had convinced myself that we had been conversing throughout the day and visiting each other at night on the inner planes. The truth was, I had not spoken a word to him or seen him for months. Was I crazy? Somewhat numb from these realizations, I mustered the courage to call my former boyfriend to confess what I had been doing on the so-called inner planes since we had parted. He was speechless and his response confirmed my worst fears. No, he had not thought of me, or felt anything for me, for months. Humiliated and shamed, I apologized and asked for his forgiveness and prayers.

Clearly, I had been deluded. If my essence twin hadn't been my constant companion, who was it that *had* been with me in my self-created delusion? Fear, confusion and despair followed. What had taken me down such a misguided path? I was not destined to be with my essence twin after all. Did essence twins really exist? That night, I gave up my fantasy life and let go of my hopes for an essence twin. Like an alcoholic who has hit rock bottom, I felt a terrible void. Suicidal, I called friends to ask if I could stay with them until my feelings of despair lifted.

At this critical fork in the road, I vowed to God I would not allow myself to ever become obsessed with any man in such a fashion again. Whatever mistakes I had made as I wandered through my life's journey, one thing remained central: I truly and deeply loved God and desired to know the truth about His purposes for me. For the first time in my career as a channel, I began to question the integrity of my inner world, my fellow channels, our guides and the information being given to us. Come to think of it, I had seen others go through similar experiences with their essence twins. They had spent months, even years, chasing after their elusive twin, until they arrived at a dead end. How could others have directed me to pursue my desires in such an inappropriate manner? Who could I trust to tell me the truth? What was the truth?

Chapter 12

Ascended Masters and Initiations of the Soul

During this period when I was simultaneously involved with Tibetan Buddhism and pursuing my essence twin, I came across the esoteric and Gnostic teachings of Alice Bailey. Alice Bailey was a channel that lived in the early part of the 20th century and was a leader in the occult movement during that period. Gnosticism was nothing new, of course. It had begun as a heresy in the earliest centuries of Christianity. Gnostics believe that matter is evil and that emancipation comes through gnosis or knowledge, especially secret knowledge. While I had not encountered the idea that matter was evil in Bailey's books, her teachings re-ignited my intense desire to understand the hidden secrets of the universe. Again, I hoped that this acquired knowledge would lead to my spiritual liberation.

Webster's dictionary defines esoteric as: *designed for or understood by the specially initiated alone, a body of esoteric legal doctrine, requiring or exhibiting knowledge that is restricted to a small group, difficult to understand.* Alice Bailey's books overflowed with complex formulas for healing, systems of thinking and esoteric terminology that claimed to hold the key to higher soul initiations. The source for her volumes of complex, channeled material, she said, originated with her guides, the "ascended masters," human beings who had become enlightened teachers after many lifetimes. Succeeding through a multitude of spiritual initiations, they had eventually ascended—body and soul—to higher planes. Sound familiar? This was the Michael concept again, but rather than being a collection of souls working together, the ascended masters were individuals that had reached the highest form of transcendence and ascension. According to Bailey's writings, Christ was considered to be one of many ascended masters. I found this knowledge relative to Christ to be quite exciting, since it fit in perfectly with my belief in reincarnation.

I had embraced the Eastern belief of reincarnation in my early 20s, when I started working with my guru. In the Catholic tradition, a person has only one life. Since I had forfeited any chance to redeem my life a multitude of times by my mid-20s, I had written myself off as doomed. As with many former Catholics, I was plagued by guilt and the fear of God's condemnation. Reincarnation relieved me of the guilt that often haunted me, so that it no longer seemed to have power over me. I could work on improving myself over many lifetimes until I finally got it right.

Alice Bailey's teachings also offered me a way to deal with yet another aspect of Christianity I had struggled with – the Divine, Incarnate Christ. According to her, Christ had passed through initiations of the soul as he matured spiritually, allowing him to eventually become an ascended master. I latched on to this teaching, for although I believed in God, I did not truly believe that Christ was God and man combined – one person with two natures - human and divine. Bailey's supposition that Christ was transformed as a result of a series of initiations fit my theology perfectly. Since my early teens, I had rejected the concept of a God that would voluntarily suffer and die for my sins. Why would I *want* a God that had suffered and died? I wanted to find a way to rise *above* suffering and sin, or avoid it altogether. If, on the other hand as Bailey asserted, Christ went through initiations of the soul to become divine, then I could too, with the help of Bailey and her masters. This was an opportunity to strive to be like Christ, whose teachings I had admired, but outside of Catholicism and the Christian Church, and without having to answer to a priest for my actions.

Several popular books I had read reinforced Bailey's assertion that Christ was a man or a prophet rather than God incarnate. Some of these books were about lost gospels, or fictional novels similar to the now popular *Da Vinci Code*. My favorite novel was written from a feminist world view, wherein women strictly controlled the temple of Jerusalem. This book revised the Gospel stories in this way:

- Judas (who betrayed Christ) was secretly Christ's twin brother.
- Christ was the lover of Mary Magdalene, the high priestess of the temple.
- Somehow Judas and Mary Magdalene managed to fool the Jewish elders into thinking Christ had died on the cross, when in fact he was still alive and well.
- They maneuvered his escape and in the end, all lived happily ever after thanks to the occult talents of Mary Magdalene.
- In one fell swoop – all my issues relative to Christ were seemingly resolved!

Christ escaped suffering and death—what a relief! The thought of my eventual death had always terrified me and I had obsessively hoped that I could transcend and avoid death through some sort of higher knowledge. Also, I had never quite recovered from my experiences as a Catholic child during Holy Friday. Re-experiencing Christ's Crucifixion year after year became something I dreaded. How could God die in such a cruel manner, and for *me*? I felt ill every year while participating in the Holy Friday Stations of the Cross, and it was difficult for me to enter into the Easter celebration just two days later, for I had no personal experience with the significance or truth of Christ's Resurrection or my redemption. What difference did it make to me? I didn't feel or act differently because of it, nor did anyone in my family.

As many other Catholics of my time that had fallen away from the church, I was of the opinion that the Catholic Church was oppressive and had hidden certain facts from the masses in order to control them. I read this feminist book multiple times, each time becoming more enthralled and encouraged. The true facts of Christ's life had been hidden from us. We'd been duped! No longer would I be oppressed by guilt. I was ready to find fulfillment through working with ascended masters. Passing through higher initiations of the soul, with the possibility of transcending death while being of service to others - this was my ticket to freedom!

I began practicing a new form of meditation that commenced with the "Great Invocation", the primary incantation used in Alice Bailey's teachings to invoke the presence of these ascended masters. I also employed specific visualization techniques for clearing "chakras" and different "subtle bodies" connected to the physical body, in preparation for the different levels of initiation described in Bailey's books.

My prior Eastern initiations and out-of-body experiences, combined with all my research and readings about the ascended masters, had primed me to believe in and practice Bailey's form of spirituality. When I embarked on a week-long vacation to spectacular Big Sur, I sensed I was on the verge of a new spiritual awakening. In a way, I was right, but the culmination of all my searching and metaphysical experimentation was still years away. Overlooking the cliffs of the Pacific Ocean and listening to the soothing sound of the waves, I verbalized Bailey's "The Great Invocation". As I induced myself into a meditative trance, the "ascended masters" came to me, initiated me and accepted my commitment to be of service to them for the higher good of others.

I returned home aflame with the desire to share these teachings with others. I began to incorporate and synthesize aspects of the Michael Teaching with the teachings of Alice Bailey. I created a yearlong curriculum incorporating these twin spiritual paths. With the help of a student and friend, I completed and self-published a handbook to accompany my course, *Channeling, a Bridge to Transcendence* (Volume I, *Discovery of Being*), my first book.

Chapter 13

Second Chances

Several nights after my confession to my essence twin, I had fortunately returned from the abyss of despair and I made a pact with God. "God, please help me," I prayed. "I will stop my mind chatter and fantasizing, and will no longer try to possess or control the next relationship that You see fit to give me – whenever You present this person to me – whether tomorrow, one year from now or perhaps not at all." Utterly disgusted with myself, I no longer cared if I was destined to meet someone through mystical means – a regular guy would be just fine.

Some days after I made my pledge, I arrived an hour early for a class I was teaching in Palo Alto, near Stanford University. One of my students showed up early as well, so we decided to take a walk together to pass the time. His name was Greg, and we had developed a good friendship during the past several months through my class. As we strolled and chatted, I noticed something beyond friendship that seemed to be present between us that I hadn't noticed before. I asked Greg if he felt this "something different" too? To my surprise, Greg answered that he knew from the first moment he saw me that we were going to wind up together! I had been so wrapped up in my essence twin search that I hadn't seen the forest for the trees. All this time, Greg had been patiently waiting for me to be free and notice him.

Could it be that only a few days after my pledge, God had presented me with Greg? As we compared notes about our former relationships and failures, we discovered that we had both prayed for a healthy relationship on the same day! I was stunned. I also felt as if I was being tested immediately regarding my pledge. No matter what distracting thoughts tried to invade my mind and heart, I kept my promise to God. I fought off all urges to repeat my former compulsive behaviors. When the temptation arose to imagine or predict where our relationship was going, or what it meant on some esoteric level, I'd repeat, "Trust in God" over and over again. I even stopped listening to lovesick soft rock. Old habits die hard and these thoughts pestered me for months, but eventually they subsided. I no longer worried about our past lives or our destinies, or whether he could be my essence twin. I knew that those thoughts led to delusion. I wanted a real relationship with a man who wanted to be with me, and I knew Greg wanted the same things as well.

As a former Catholic who had also fallen away from the church, Greg understood me well. In his early 20s, he had been active in the lay community associated with a mystical, somewhat New Age Christian movement, The Holy Order of Mans (HOM). Greg and his friends were as committed to their philosophy and lifestyle as I had been to EST. When his second wife decided she no longer wanted to be part of this religious community, he left the Order in an attempt to save his marriage.

Little by little, Greg fell further away not only from the Order, but also from any form of Christianity. He, too, had explored an Eastern religion, Zen. He appreciated the practice of stilling his mind. He was also an avid reader who enjoyed aspects of New Age thought, as did I. In an odd intersection of lives, I had actually known Greg's second wife—she had been one of my clients prior to my meeting Greg. In one of our channeling sessions together, I may have even supported and encouraged her as she went through the process of deciding to leave Greg! I met Greg at a later point in time, when he came to one of my classes, hoping that he might find a way to reconnect with his wife and save his marriage. My class was already underway and full, however, so I couldn't admit him to the class. Greg's marriage dissolved and months passed. When a new class opened up, Greg decided to come on his own.

As our relationship blossomed, my desire to be geographically closer to Greg grew, as did my need to distance myself from the Michael community. Th e desire to work with ascended masters was calling me, and after my essence twin fiiasco, I hoped to start anew and freely develop my own work. I made the decision to move to Marin County, a beautiful area north of San Francisco. Greg's and my relationship deepened quickly; by our sixth month together, we knew we loved each other and we combined households in Marin, along with a friend. A year later, we married and moved to our own apartment.

In the summer of 1988, Greg's son Shayne moved in with us while he was waiting to enroll the following January at UC Berkeley. Th at winter, Greg, Shayne and their ocean-loving buddies planned a ten-day surfing trip to Baja, Mexico, hoping to catch some waves before Shayne began the daily grind of classes. With their "men only" trip in the offing, what was I going to do for ten days by myself? We joke about it now - the beginning of my next important life change occurred because of a surfing safari! While they rode the roiling tides of Baja, I would return to Europe to visit my Italian family and French friends.

I couldn't wait to see Claire in France, who despite the doctor's prediction, was still living and thriving six years after her diagnosis of terminal cancer. During that time, Claire and Sam had developed a series of seminars based on what she had learned while battling cancer. I was astonished and delighted to hear about the wonderful work they were offering to others, especially to families and cancer patients.

After we spent some time together catching up, Claire made the observation: "It seems as if you aren't present in your body". Startled, I asked her what she meant by this. "I need you to do some inner questioning and preparation before I can answer your question," Claire responded. "Write down your thoughts and reactions to specific questions I will give you and then we can talk." She assigned someone to help me that day, Nathalie, a young woman who worked on her staff. Claire dealt my ego yet another blow. How was a 19 year-old girl going to help me? My pride was more than slightly bruised.

Throughout the day, I labored over Claire's written questions with Nathalie at my side. I nodded off frequently, as was my norm. This pattern of falling asleep while examining my life had started and persisted throughout my work in EST. In one 6-day intensive seminar, if the EST seminar leaders caught us dozing, they would ask us to stand up and hold a log over our heads. I did my share of log holding—thankfully, none of them hit my head! After an introspective day monitored by Nathalie, I reviewed my notes and realized that my life was not the paradise I thought it to be.

What did these questions and answers reveal to me? I discovered that I had cloaked my egocentric attitudes and unhealthy habits under a carefully crafted image, that of the "New Age Spiritual Teacher." The problem was, wherever I went, there I was, and unhealthy patterns from prior relationships were already beginning to resurface in my marriage with Greg. This time, I really wanted my marriage to work, but I felt at a loss as to how to deal with our deeper issues. I was also worried about my stepson, our finances and my health.

Claire spent the next few days relentlessly and patiently working with me, as she helped me discover the roots of my destructive thinking patterns. It took a while, but I began to soften and shed some healing tears. As we progressed, I sensed a shift in my being. It was as if, at least for a brief period of time, I stepped out of a fog and glimpsed how life would be if I could stay "in my body." (Being out of one's body is a term that I learned in my channeling classes – it refers to living in a disconnected way, in denial or not being fully present). Indeed, I had been on a cloud, daydreaming my way through life, with my guides for companions. I wore a headset and listened to New Age music or Hindu mantras much of the time, numbly avoiding reality. Somehow, Claire managed to pull me out of the ethers and wake me up. Thankful for this new sense of life and alertness, I asked her if she could come to California to lead one of her seminars the following summer. It was a leap of faith, since I had no idea how I would pull this off. At the time, I also didn't comprehend what inviting Claire and Sam to California would mean, and how it would end up changing all of our lives. I just knew that because of what I had experienced, I wanted to bring Claire, Sam and their staff to my home turf for more.

Chapter 14

From Confusion to Clarity

On my plane ride back to California, I reflected on my five intense and life changing days with Claire. I had to admit to myself that I was not living a real or truthful life. Claire was right, I really wasn't living "in my body", in the present. Claire knew something I didn't. She had fought long and hard to recover from the darkest of times in order to rebuild her life and her relationships. Inspired by her example, I optimistically looked forward to accomplishing miracles with my newly changed self. My high hopes for a new life faded quickly, however, as I dove back into the daily grind of life back home.

I didn't completely forget, however. I took a few steps toward putting together the promised seminar with Claire, although how I would actually sponsor and direct this four-day workshop over two weekends in August, I wasn't sure. My clients were intrigued. "Are we going to be channeling?" they asked. "No", I replied.

"What are we going to be doing?" they queried. "I'm not sure," I said, "but it will be intense."

"How late did you say this workshop would go?" they wanted to know. "Oh, maybe until 10 p.m. or midnight!" I replied.

"Who is the person leading it?" "A French Holocaust and cancer survivor," I explained.

My regular students didn't know what to think. The proposed workshop did not quite fit in with ascended masters and channeling, our usual topics. Although I sensed that they were all interested in meeting Claire and her family, I knew that my vague descriptions of spending twelve or more hours a day together for four days, pursuing a new and perhaps less sensational topic, weren't helping my sales pitch.

After four months of publicity, only one person had signed up and given me a deposit for the August seminar. I had thirteen people's airline tickets, a hotel conference room and multiple other expenses to cover! By mid-June I was ready to jump ship. I called Sam and Claire, proposing that we just host a couple of informative evenings and perhaps a one-day event. They could come for a vacation instead. "No one wants to do a four-day workshop," I insisted. "OK," responded Claire stubbornly. "If you don't want to do four days, maybe we could do three days with a sleepover instead!" This wasn't what I wanted to hear. We went back and forth for some time as I insisted that I couldn't pull it together and we needed to change our plans. Eventually, I erupted angrily, frustrated that I couldn't persuade them to my point of view. By this time, we'd been on our transcontinental phone call for an hour. Sam gently asked me, "Polly, what are you afraid of?" I burst into tears. "I don't remember why I committed to bring you to America. I don't tt know why I'm doing this. I don't want to lose you as friends, but why am I doing this?"

Unhinged, I couldn't stop crying. I was afraid of my commitment, fearful of what keeping it would mean to me, and troubled about how it would affect my reputation as a successful teacher. Despite the stormy call, Sam and Claire acted as true friends. Sam ended the call saying, "We can't force you to keep your commitment, but if you choose to trust us and honor your word, your life will change."

I hung up the phone on them, still sobbing. I ran to Greg, who had heard most of the conversation. "I don't know why I'm doing this? Can you help me?" I pleaded with him.

"I thought you wanted to change your life and the lives of others. Isn't that what you experienced when you were with Sam and Claire in France? I remember how different you were when you first returned home. Don't you remember?" I pondered his words, searched my heart and finally said, "Yes, yes, I remember now. I wanted my life and our lives to be better. I did feel different for a while. That's why I wanted to bring them to America. I remember how I felt. I wanted to have that feeling again and sustain it. That's why I'm doing this! I wanted to have others around me experience this feeling too. Oh, I remember! Yes, thank you!"

Something shifted in my approach to the seminar as I began to recall my experiences in Paris and how they had helped me. Other people noticed my increased enthusiasm, even if I still couldn't tell them exactly what we would be doing together for four days. Within six weeks, I had managed to enroll forty other people – even Greg agreed to attend!

Then my French friends arrived – all twelve of them – to stay with us. Twelve French folks descending on my three-bedroom apartment was, in itself, a life changing experience! The workshop, in spite of all my fears and considerations, turned out to a success. We learned so much together - about changing bad habits, about choosing to make life and others good, about honoring commitments and setting new goals. A little more of me returned to my body and woke up once again. During the workshop, Claire suggested that one seminar was not enough. "Change takes time to integrate. We need time and some sort of business framework to continue the work we've started together in the United States."

After much discussion and brainstorming, several of us came up with the idea to form a non-profit organization. The volunteers would form a non-profit entity that would bring Claire and Sam to the U.S. three or four times a year. Little did our small band of committed volunteers know what we were getting ourselves into! Six weeks after our first seminar, Sam and Claire called me. They hadn't heard from me since they had returned to France and we had another seminar planned for November. "How are you Polly? "Not great!" "What is happening?" "Not much!" I had retreated into my cave again, completely overwhelmed with how to manage volunteers and enroll people, let alone establish a non-profit organization. They gave me a pep talk and we started to set up weekly overseas support calls with our volunteer staff, consisting mostly of my clients and friends. Talk about meetings that went nowhere and lasted for hours!

In the midst of our transcontinental planning sessions, the 1989 Loma Prieta earthquake struck in California. During that same period of time, Claire had developed a severe glaucoma in her right eye. Her friends and family in France thought she was absolutely nuts to visit the San Francisco Bay Area one week after the earthquake. Undeterred, Claire and company arrived to the rolling motion of aftershocks. Somehow, we had managed to sign up over fifty people to attend our workshop, which we held in semi-darkness as the subdued lighting mitigated the severe eye pain Claire experienced when exposed to even minimal amounts of light. We forged our way through the first few months, and then years, of our fledgling organization, as we continued to fly Sam, Claire and their staff from Paris to San Francisco several times a year.

In spite of all our mishaps and challenges, we had a great time together. One summer, several of us decided to become housemates. We rented a large house in Tiburon, a bayside village just north of San Francisco, with a pool and a wonderful view. To add to the chaos, we moved our non-profit office into our home as well. We lived on a quiet street with mostly elderly neighbors. Our lease specifically limited the number of visitors we could have for a variety of reasons, one being that we used our own septic system rather than the town utility. I had attempted several times, unsuccessfully, to convey this limitation to our staff in France; instead, I was informed that 25-30 people were going to be staying with us for our August seminar! In desperation, I rented an RV and two outhouses which were hidden from view.

The French then invaded Tiburon! We might have gotten away with all our visitors had Claire not decided to host a guest event at our house after the workshop. When one hundred people decided to attend our guest event/party, we scrambled to sign up volunteers to park the guests' cars, rented a loudspeaker system and moved all the furniture out of our large living room onto the deck. The successful event went on for hours. It should not have been a surprise when our neighbors panicked!

The next day, while all our friends rested by the pool, our leasing agent stormed up the stairs and rang our doorbell. Claire opened the door in her bikini sweetly saying, "Bonjour!" In the background, our agent could see multitudes of people jumping in the pool and laughing. "What the .... are you doing here? Do you know how many complaints I have had?" she fumed. "You better have a good explanation for all of this or your lease will be terminated! What are the toilets doing outside?

What about all the traffic and noise?" It was some sort of miracle that Claire and I managed to talk our way out of this looming catastrophe. From that point on, I developed recurring ulcers each time the French staff stayed at our house. They did return for subsequent visits, but only as a group of 10, instead of the 25-30 that stayed that one eventful summer. We had achieved probationary status, however. The landlord's son frequently drove past the house, peering up at our windows in the early morning to see if we were behaving ourselves!

Over time, my private practice and classes changed as I continued to work with Sam and Claire. About fifty percent of my students and friends participated in the programs they facilitated, and many of them became the volunteer backbone of our non-profit organization. I divided my work almost equally between my private practice and our non-profit enterprise. As I became more organized and grounded, so did my work, and as a result, so did many of my students. I incorporated many of Sam and Claire's techniques related to working on one's ego into my classes and private sessions with great results.

In my work with Sam and Claire, one of the issues we worked on intensively was understanding reactive mechanisms. That fateful evening on the phone, when I erupted in anger with Claire and Sam, forced me to think about how often my reactions controlled me. I came to understand that my unconscious beliefs formed the foundation of my ego, and were at the root of all the instances when I had overreacted to someone or something. It was challenging and gut-wrenching to realize that my reactions and false beliefs controlled my life, not me. Regrettably, I often wasn't able to reign in my reactions until after I had I had created unfortunate damage in my relationships.

I began to ask myself: is part of my longing to transcend my current lifetime simply a desire to escape or an immature reaction to something in my life that I want to avoid? Could my seemingly higher spiritual goals be rooted in these kinds of escapist emotions, rather than some spiritual quest for truth? How could I truly know? At times, I could be unreliable and untrustworthy. I struggled to let those who loved me, and who understood my knee-jerk tendency toward avoidance, to challenge me. "What do you mean I can't be trusted?" "What do you mean you cannot depend on me?" "Go away!" I would cry. "Leave me alone." How many times had I blamed others, erupted in anger and then left them?

How many friendships over the years did I see go down the drain? How often had I been sick in body and soul? The costs of my dysfunctional life were extensive and sobering.

Since I did not want to have my reactions be the source of my decisions in life, I promised myself that I would struggle to control them, rather than giving in to my desire to lash out at others and run. I could see that I had a predisposition to trust my internal world and my reactions more than my closest friends. One day Claire asked me, "Why do you trust your guides more than me or other people who love you?" Over the course of my work with Sam and Claire, I realized that I had made countless decisions that I later regretted based not only on my reactions, but also on questionable information that I had received from other channels or from my own personal meditations.

These thoughts and questions shook me to the core. Perhaps my channeling, or the channeling of others, could be inaccurate at times? Perhaps some of my inner guidance was just my own subconscious mind rationalizing my desire for escape? I was not sure what to do with these ponderings. At stake was my lifetime of work and study. I resolved to trust Claire, hoping that in time I would find answers to my questions about the integrity of channeling and of my spiritual sources.

I had to have escape hatches in my life. I would alternate between feeling trapped and inspired, wanting to escape and then desiring to stay. Sam and Claire, however, persisted. Slowly but surely, they closed my back doors when I could not. A deep bond of trust formed between us; I knew I could count on the integrity of my French friends. I, in turn, wanted to be reliable for them, and for my husband and my family. I couldn't just abandon all that we had started – although at times I tried. Knowing I was a tough nut to crack, God sent me a Holocaust survivor and her band of comrades!

As the years passed, I noticed that many of my worst patterns, such as being irresponsible with money, unreliable in relationships or getting sick to avoid a challenging situation, were changing. My stepson was doing much better and my marriage felt as if it were going to last. Even though healing had occurred in so many of these areas, I still struggled at times with the desire to run from life and reality. This puzzled me to the point where I prayed for several months for an answer. A response came to me in a most unlikely manner when I went to see the movie

The Prince of Tides. The plot revolves around a man who has problems in his relationships and seeks the help of a therapist. During the course of the movie, he begins to remember and relive his experiences of sexual abuse. When I walked out of the theater, a little voice in my heart said, "There is more to the incident with JS than you remember". My heart started racing and my stomach turned.

JS was a boy from my childhood. When I was nine years old, my parents left my sister and me for the weekend in the care of my aunt Louise. While playing outside, JS asked me, "Do you want to play with me and have fun?" "Sure," I said. We often played with other kids – what could be the harm? My mother had frequently cautioned me about playing with boys alone, but this day I disregarded her admonition to me. What my family and I had remembered about this later, was that JS had exposed himself to me and scared me. I started crying and screaming loud enough that my aunt heard me. She called my name several times and I returned crying.

I decided to consult a therapist who specialized in sexual abuse. She slowly led me back through the incident. When I began to relive the encounter with JS in therapy, my body started to shake violently and I felt nauseated and terrified. Continuing with her questioning, my therapist guided me to relive the rest of the incident. I remembered, much to my shock, that I had been raped. I kept asking myself, "How could I have not known about this, or not remembered what really happened?" My experience relived felt unnatural and surreal because I didn't initially feel emotionally connected to what I was reliving. I felt as if I were watching from the outside, narrating a story, and I wanted to jump off the couch and run, run, run.

My nine months of therapy culminated with a bout of illness while vacationing at Lake Tahoe over Labor Day weekend. When I returned home, I went to see my mom. She had supported me to pursue therapy when my memories first surfaced. I had waited to share what I remembered with her until I felt calmer. During our visit, she revealed that the incident had happened over a Labor Day weekend — and of course, my parents had been in Lake Tahoe! No wonder I was so ill! My mom then filled in parts of the story I could not have known. She realized that I had changed after the rape, but no one had really wanted to believe at the time that this had truly happened. We both experienced a profound healing and cried in each other's arms.

I had spent thirty years living in fear and blame, pushing others away and running when life became too intense. No wonder I retreated into my inner world. I had been sexually abused not long after my initial spiritual awakening and subsequent desire to be a nun were stifled. My hopes as a young Catholic girl of serving God in purity died at the age of nine. No wonder I trusted my guides more than people.

Until my late 20s, I had a recurring nightmare where a monster was chasing me. Every time I had this nightmare, it would persist throughout the night, and I would wake up exhausted. I cleverly evaded this monster, just barely escaping his clutches, but I never felt safe. In a dream class, my instructor counseled me to stand my ground, stop running and see what happened. He even asked me to make friends with the monster. I followed his instructions—I stood my ground and talked to the monster until he turned into a flower. The dream stopped recurring, but I kept running in my conscious life for another ten years. Now at the age of thirty-nine, I could finally stop running. I had identified the monster.

So many of my irrational behaviors and entrenched habits now made sense to me. I didn't know what would be required of me to fulfill my new desire to take responsibility for my life, but I'd been brought back to reality and had survived my landing. If I felt the urge to run in the future, I knew I could now stand my ground.

Part II
The Battle for My Soul

Chapter 1

Greg's Epiphany

Although creating the non-profit company with Sam and Claire had kept us busy and fulfilled, Greg had been struggling for several years with his spiritual life. Although he was a good mentor and teacher and we worked well together, something was missing in our seminars for Greg, and as time passed he became increasingly restless. Finally, he told me he did not want to continue participating in our programs. I was torn. How would his departure impact our organization and more importantly, our marriage? He thought the best solution would be for me to stop my participation as well, but I still felt engaged and committed. In my new resolve to be more consistent and reliable, I believed I should continue the work with Sam and Claire. By this time, we had weathered many changes together and our commitment to our marriage was unwavering, so I also felt that we would survive together, even if we were not doing the same things. Nonetheless, Greg's decision to leave the work presented a unique challenge for both of us.

At the same time, Greg also left his profession as a chiropractor. When we met, he was just completing his studies in chiropractic school, but after five years in private practice, he realized that he was not happy in his work. Souls needed healing, not just bodies, and even as he helped people through chiropractic treatment, he could see that he could only partially help them. Patients often didn't want to take personal responsibility for their healing process. After all, he was the doctor – wasn't it his job to make them better? Adding to Greg's disillusionment was the competitive aspect of attracting new clients, the skyrocketing cost of malpractice insurance and the endless stream of paperwork. Now 40-something and pondering how to remedy his career crisis, Greg recalled aptitude tests he had taken in his early 20s, which indicated that he would make a good park ranger. One of Greg's friends, a park ranger, encouraged Greg to become a gardener. He loved being outside and working with his hands, so it seemed like a good fit. He bought a funky old pick-up truck and some yard maintenance equipment and mailed out postcards advertising his services. Lo and behold, within six months he was making more money than he'd ever made as a chiropractor!

With his career change, at least the financial aspect of our marriage was finally working. I continued my therapeutic work and seminars, and for a time, we began to live somewhat separate spiritual lives. I had my work with Claire, my private practice and the support of other colleagues during these years of intense and extended seminar and class schedules. Greg had little spiritual and emotional support other than the consolation of nature, which he experienced in his gardening work and surfing trips.

Lonely, and at a loss as to what to do with his life, Greg initially filled his free time with reading war novels and playing paint ball games. He bought combat fatigue outfits and paintball equipment and guns. The irony of our situation now makes me laugh. While I was working for peace with a holocaust survivor, Greg was playing war games! During the weekends when I was in seminars, Greg was in outdoor paint ball battles. I didn't know what to make of his new hobby. As an avid sportsman and big kid at heart, Greg found paint ball to be a good way to blow off steam. But I could see that he was struggling with depression and filling his void with the thrill of war games.

This phase of Greg's life lasted for a couple of years and then he seemed to settle down. The war games and novels disappeared and in their place, a prayer corner appeared in our bedroom. To my utter surprise, Greg said that his restlessness had led him to consider returning to "a traditional Christian religion." Before I could stop myself, I exclaimed "What do you mean you want to be part of a traditional

Christian religion? Are you nuts?" Hadn't we both walked away from Catholicism? Greg took my reactions in stride, avoiding further conflict, but I started noticing even more of a change in him. He was no longer depressed.

Out of the blue, Greg proposed that we go away for a few days to Stinson Beach. There in our beachside motel, my husband confided in me the secret of his change. He began by thanking me for upholding my commitment to stay with my work with Sam and Claire while I supported him through his struggles and changes. "I know I haven't been easy to live with the last few years," he said. "I realize now that if you had abandoned your commitment, I would never have found mine."

"What do you mean?" I asked.

"Do you remember how I told you that I left my Christian community because my wife no longer wanted to be involved, and I was afraid that I would lose her?" he queried.

I said yes, I remembered that. "When you didn't leave your work with Claire for me, I became quite angry at you and Claire, but I didn't know why," he continued.

"I know," I said. The truth was, Greg hadn't even been speaking to Claire, an awkward situation that I had somehow managed to navigate. Greg went on, "When I broke my commitment to my religious community for my wife, I unknowingly started walking away from God. If you hadn't kept your commitment with Claire, I wouldn't have come to this realization."

Deeply moved, I tearfully replied, "You have no idea how much what you've said means to me. You know how much I've been fighting to stay true to my commitments to others."

With tears in his eyes, Greg said, "During the last few months, I finally realized that I was sick in soul and had fallen into a deep depression. As a chiropractor, I knew my depression would eventually affect the health of my body. I felt as if I were on the brink of hell. I was spiritually dying and I knew that if I did not change my life, I would die a premature death."

"I knew you were in a desperate state!" I cried. "But I felt so powerless these last couple of years to help you."

Greg wasn't done. "I saw how I'd been throwing my life away. At the same time, I realized that I wanted to be of use to society. I wanted to play my part in passing on something of value to the next generation. I became acutely aware in a moment of truth that my life was nothing without God." He paused.

"Go on," I said, hanging on to his every word now.

"This realization, however, was still not sufficient to lift me out of my abyss. Rather, it propelled me onto my knees," Greg looked at me, expecting a reaction.

"What happened then?" I asked.

"A beacon of hope entered my heart and comforted me," he said. "In that moment, I realized something profoundly life-altering about God."

"What was that?" I asked, hardly able to contain myself.

"I'm not sure you will understand this, Polly. In fact, what I'm going to say next may trigger you," Greg whispered. I could see that he was struggling to share the conclusion of his epiphany with me. "I don't care," I said. "You've changed. Whatever it is, I'll deal with it, because it's changed you for the better. I love you."

Reassured, Greg continued. "I understood that Jesus Christ was truly the Son of God, and that He became man to show us how to live a life devoted to God."

For once, I managed to remain silent as I pondered his words in my heart. Greg continued. "In that moment, I went from thinking about God to believing in Him again. This was the most profound spiritual awakening of my life." Without reacting negatively, I just sat there in tears, rejoicing. I was so moved by his confession, his humility of heart and his return to life. Joy filled us both.

Throughout the weekend, we continued to talk. Greg said he prayed about what to do with the emerging warmth in his heart towards God. The answer that came to him was that he ought to begin where he had left off fifteen years before, when he had walked away from his Christian community. He had reconnected with some of his old friends and to his surprise, his former community had gone through their own transition and awakening.

He discovered that his former community, the Holy Order of Mans (HOM) as it was originally conceived and practiced, no longer existed.

He also learned that over 2,000 members of his former community had changed its name to 'Christ the Savior Brotherhood' when they decided to join the Eastern Orthodox Church.[3] I didn't even know what the Eastern Orthodox Church was, but it had 'Eastern' in its title so that was encouraging! Apparently, their newly named brotherhood still had parishes, now Orthodox Christian churches, in many of the urban and rural cities where the former HOM communities once existed. Most of the former priests became ordained priests in the Eastern Church. Some married, while others became monks or nuns, and they labored to build several of the first Eastern Orthodox Monasteries in the U.S. that were founded by Americans. Greg was amazed to hear about all the changes. He was also so relieved by my curious and intrigued response to his sharing that he mustered up the courage to ask me to go to church with him.

As an adult, I had been in Catholic churches to attend my niece's baptism, to pay respects at a relative's funeral or to attend a friend's wedding, but I hadn't considered those occasions "going to church". I still harbored anger, suspicion, resentments and judgments about the Catholic Church, and Christianity in general. I would set those emotions aside to support a friend or a family member's special event, but going purposefully to any church in order to participate in Christian worship was the farthest thing from my mind or heart. Yet, I truly rejoiced for my husband and I wanted to meet his friends and see firsthand what they were experiencing.

The following Sunday, we entered a small Eastern Orthodox chapel in the basement of a Victorian house in San Francisco. It was during Lent, so everything was shrouded in black and the chapel resembled a cave. Greg seemed to be quite at ease during the service. I, however, within thirty unbearable minutes, ran out of the chapel, crying hysterically! This brief amount of time in this unassuming, sweet little chapel had triggered an emotional explosion in me I was not prepared for - the music, the candles, the icons, the portrayals of Christ and the saints, even the way people were attired, all contributed to a massive, uncontrollable reaction within me. "I have to get out of here or I'll suffocate!" I exclaimed as I fled the chapel, the pastor's wife running after me. Greg took it all in stride — he knew me pretty well by then.

"It's okay. Polly will process her emotions and come back after a while. She's just in reaction," Greg said calmly, to the amazement of all.

Had I not worked with Sam and Claire for years on understanding and controlling my reactive mechanisms, I would not have returned. I hiked to a park at the top of a nearby hill and sat sobbing for a good thirty minutes. However, despite my considerable resistance, I returned to join the parishioners for lunch. I knew my reactions were unhealthy so I didn't want to walk away from them. Something in me needed to heal – a lot of something, apparently.

I also sensed how important Greg's emerging faith was for him. I wanted to support him, and my own healing, so I told him I would accompany him to church at least once a month for six months. If this was to be Greg's new spiritual path, I wanted to learn how to go to church with him without reacting so strongly to it. I also had to admit that I liked participating in something spiritual with Greg again.

While I struggled along in my once-a -month visits, Greg jumped into a multitude of opportunities offered by his church community. He frequently went to visit St. Paisius Eastern Orthodox Monastery in Forestville, about an hour's drive north from where we lived, which offered lectures, retreats, services and fellowship in a serene, secluded setting. I remained at home, teaching classes and conducting workshops with Sam and Claire.

Greg had majored in art during his four years in college, but he had stopped his creative work years before we met. When he prayed in church before icons of the saints, however, he was inspired to rekindle his art through an iconography course offered at the monastery. In his free time, Greg began painting icons of saints. Initially, he created six unique icons utilizing a combination of wood burning and oil paint.

One of these icons was of Blessed John of Shanghai and San Francisco[4]. Greg wanted to finish it before Blessed John's canonization which was scheduled to take place on July 2, 1994, in the Russian Orthodox Cathedral on Geary Street in San Francisco. The canonization of a Saint is a once-in-a-lifetime event, especially in the United States. Greg was planning to attend this extraordinary all-day service in San Francisco at the Holy Virgin Cathedral, which St. John had labored for years to build. I wanted to go to the services with Greg, but I knew my back would not be able to bear the long hours of standing.

Greg returned from the long canonization day filled with awe. He couldn't comprehend how he managed to stand for twelve hours while the prayers and singing flowed in a ceaseless stream. The entire day was grace-filled and intensely powerful for him, so much so that soon after Blessed John's canonization, Greg announced he wanted to become a catechumen.

A catechumen is the term given to someone who decides to prepare him or herself for entry into the Eastern Orthodox Church. There is a special prayer and blessing one receives to begin one's active study to become an Orthodox Christian. Greg said that the priest had mentioned that I could participate in this process and receive this blessing as well. I was torn about what to do. True, I was reacting less negatively to church as time went on, but I wasn't even close to being as committed as Greg for this next step.

The morning of this special blessing, I was reading an Orthodox book about Mary, the Mother of God, written by St. John. In the midst of my confusion, the soft, sweet presence of the Mother of God surrounded me for a moment, as it had once before when I was a child. She spoke to my heart and made me feel safe. I felt as if Mary were saying, "Trust me, you'll be okay and this will be good for you." The experience, although less intense, was as real as the visitation I had experienced as a young girl on retreat. Through all my years of wandering, I had somehow managed to retain my trust in Mary—my heart was still open to her. I went ahead and received the blessing, becoming a catechumen with Greg that day.

I continued to go to church with Greg for three more months. However, I couldn't picture making my own path in Eastern Orthodox Christianity. I was really going to Church more to be with Greg than to be with God, and so I chose for a time to discontinue going to church on a regular basis.

For years, Greg had supported me in doing my work with Sam and Claire, even though he was no longer participating in our programs. I knew I had to support him now in his spiritual goals, even if I were not by his side. I was sad that we were not sharing the same spiritual life, but our non-profit organization was starting to make plans to go to Auschwitz in the summer of 1995. My commitment to this mission began consuming all my time, while Greg's growing faith took much of his free time.

In the fall of 1994, Greg attended a conference at St. Paisius Monastery where clergy and lay people from the brotherhood gathered from all over the United States to study and pray together. Someone asked Greg if he could give a priest a ride to the airport on his way home, and Greg agreed. The priest in question, Fr. Simeon, asked if they could stop to visit Blessed John's incorrupt body on the way. Greg reported that the grace-filled energy of the saint's relics radiated throughout the Cathedral. The entire experience of the retreat, his talk with Fr. Simeon and the visit to the church had profoundly moved him. But that wasn't all the story.

Greg had been unsuccessfully nursing a large, ugly wart on one of his fingers for twenty years. I would frequently urge him to remove it, until Greg finally confessed to me. "I have this secret prayer. I've been waiting for it to be healed. I've been hoping that when I find the right spiritual path for me, that it will disappear, as my sign that I've finally arrived where God wanted me to be." The morning after his weekend conference and visit to Blessed John's tomb, he woke to find the wart gone and his finger returned to normal. We were both astounded. It was a miracle! Greg felt so blessed to have his prayer finally answered.

During an extended vigil service at the St. Paisius Monastery several months later, Greg witnessed another miracle related to St. John. In the middle of the evening prayers, the priest anointed a young man in the community who had a severe cancer on his face. The oil the priest used was taken from a special container that rested at the feet of St. John's relics. The young man later reported that he experienced a burning sensation on the anointed side of his face that persisted throughout the service. When he emerged from prayers, the cancer was gone! This second miracle was confirmation for Greg that he had truly found the right path.

That spring before we went to Auschwitz, Greg was baptized. Observing my husband through the months preceding and following his baptism, I marveled at the changes I saw in him. He was softer, calmer, more patient and more loving. I had never seen him so peaceful or at home with himself.

Chapter 2

My Initial Struggles
With Eastern Orthodox
Christianity

Greg had found his spiritual home and he was at peace. I couldn't say the same for me. I recalled my reaction to my first Eastern Orthodox service that I attended with Greg. We had walked in during the prayers before communion. The bleak effect of everything being enshrouded in Lenten black or purple, combined with the heavy smell of incense and the cave-like ambiance of the chapel, had overwhelmed me. Then I began repeatedly hearing words such as "sin", "sinner" and "repent". Every one of my unresolved and lingering issues with the Catholic Church surfaced within minutes. I felt suffocated, guilty, wrong, betrayed, angry, fearful, lonely, separate, embarrassed and nauseated. Within thirty minutes, I exclaimed to Greg, "I have to get out of here!" and ran out of the chapel, the pastor's wife in pursuit.

"Are you okay?" she had asked. "No, no, not right now. Please just leave me alone," I replied frantically. At first I ran, then slowed to a walk as I trudged up a steep hill to the top of Buena Vista Park, where I collapsed under a tree and sobbed.

My mind raced. "I need to get hold of myself! What an idiot I am! How stupid I must have looked! What is the matter with me? I hate church! I'm not a sinner! I'm not wrong! I'm not bad! Oh, what have I gotten myself into?" My reactions spilled forth for many minutes before

I was able to calm down. After all the work I had done with Sam and Claire to learn how to better control my over-reactive personality, I realized in that moment that I had a choice. Would I be willing to look at *why* I was reacting with such hostility to the church and Christianity, or would I never walk into a church service with Greg again?

In the past, I would have solely blamed the church for my negative feelings, without taking any responsibility for my reactions. This time was different. I was too well trained now to simply cut and run. Besides, too much was at stake. For Greg's sake and my own sanity, I knew I had to confront the demons of my religious past. I reluctantly, but determinedly, walked down the hill and rejoined Greg and his friends in the dining room. Everyone was quite kind to me. I apologized and ate a little food, but I was unable to talk about what happened and we left soon after.

I struggled for days after that visit, but I didn't run from my fears. Instead, I told Greg I'd go back for another church service, but not for a month. During that time, with Greg's support, I spent the entire month working through my initial reactions to what I had heard in Church. Greg sought the support of his friends, who helped him help me. Greg's patience with his semi-hysterical wife amazed me then and amazes me still.

He began by reframing and explaining the meaning of the religious words that had so upset me. We started with the loaded word *sin*. How I hated that word, and how guilty it always made me feel—I'd run from it like the plague. But what is sin? To my surprise, I learned that sin is not just a state of being devoid of grace or goodness; according to the Greek meaning, to sin is *to miss the mark*, to lose our connection with love. To be a *sinner* meant that I had separated myself from others and God. I had stepped away from love. This reminded me of some of the concepts that I had studied with Sam and Claire.

The next word I needed to understand anew was *disobedience*. I learned that the root of the word "obey" comes from Latin, oboe dire, *to listen to; ob, to or toward + audire, to hear*. When we do not *listen to* our conscience, we are choosing to enter a state of separation or sin. It had been my disobedience, my lack of listening to God and my conscience, that had caused pain and suffering for myself and others, time and time again.

Next, Greg explained the meaning of the word *repentance*. In my work with Claire, I had learned that when our pride gets the best of us, we often choose to justify and continue our egotistical actions, insisting that we are "right" and others are "wrong". When we don't perceive the consequences of our inappropriate thoughts and actions, pride continues to run the show. But if we regret our selfish actions, and experience a change of mind and heart that moves us back towards goodness and love, then we enter into a state of repentance. I discovered that I had been striving for repentance for years without really knowing it!

Armed with these more clarified definitions, I was ready to go back to church for the next round in my efforts to become more neutral towards Christianity. This time, however, I hadn't even arrived at the parish front door before the mental battle had begun again. On the way to church, I began to remember the priests I had known as a child. One of them had yelled at me several times while I was in the confessional when I was perhaps ten or eleven years old. He also scolded my sister and me in front of everyone in church for attending the wrong mass! His actions had driven me away from that parish. Those incidents, along with my negative experiences during my years in Catholic schools, became a toxic brew of bitter memories. By my late teens, my heart had hardened. If I saw Christians behaving unkindly, I would add hypocrisy to my list of reasons of why the Church and Christianity were wrong. As the years passed, my list grew.

Of course, Greg had heard all the above, and more, from me. He must have wondered, as he brought me back to church, what I would do this time. Fortunately, when I entered the chapel the second time, my thoughts quieted down within a few minutes. To my surprise, I managed to stay in church for the entire service. I listened to the prayers and actually relaxed a little. Afterwards, we stayed for lunch and I engaged in pleasant conversations with people. What a breakthrough!

When we got back into the car, however, my reactions began again. This pattern continued each time I went to church. While I stood in church, I would be calm and relatively peaceful. However, for hours before and after the service, I would struggle with the things I didn't like—or even hated—about Christianity. Frequently, I would pound the dashboard of our car in anger.

"Christians bomb abortion clinics!"

"Christian missionaries abused native peoples and destroyed their cultures!"

"They launched the Crusades, the Inquisition and witch burnings!"

"Look at all the sexual misconduct by members of the clergy!"

"And how about the way women have been treated in the church?"

"And what about the misuse of power and wealth by members of the clergy?"

During my conversations with others at the church, I appreciated how people really listened to me. We would enter into lively but serious discussions that would generally end in laughter. We eventually agreed that most of the behaviors I cited above did not fall into the category of true Christian behavior, but rather existed due to the fallen state of humanity.

My reactions to fundamentalist and evangelical Christians surfaced as well. Their missionary methods unfortunately brought out the worst in me. *Jesus saves! Repent, the end is at hand! If you are not baptized, you will go to hell.* If I had dishes to spare, I would have broken them over the heads of people who said these things! How dare these Christians presume they know the state of my soul or other souls! My mind would seethe for hours. To my relief, I learned that Orthodox Christians don't use these methods of evangelizing.

Some of my other questions Greg referred to the priest to handle. "If God is good, why does He allow bad things to happen to good people? Why is there war? Can't God just stop war before everyone gets all worked up and people get hurt? If God truly is love, why would He allow us to be so miserable? If God really heard our prayers, why don't we get the answer we want right away? If God is present everywhere and resides in all things and knows all things – past, present and future – how could he let us suffer? "

Our priest was up to the challenge. "We have 'free will'," he explained. "We have the God given ability to choose. We can choose, and do choose, to do things that are not for our highest good." I had worked for years with Sam and Claire on this challenge and our ability to make rational, clear choices for good. I had experienced the consequences and costs of my ego-based choices, which I had made from selfishness, blame, judgment and resentment.

He continued, "Perhaps the universe did not just spit us out? What if we are made in the image and likeness of a Divine Being called God?" Even in my most alienated moments, when I declared that the universe was in charge, I did not truly believe it. In my heart and soul, I didn't really believe that an impersonal universe had created *me*, a human being. I was listening.

"Human suffering started with 'The Fall'," he added, "with Adam and Eve and original sin. Whether one understands Adam and Eve in a literal or a symbolic sense, we can all agree that something went wrong in Paradise and that human existence is plagued by this fall from grace even now. We are all seeking paradise lost. We struggle to feel secure, to love and be loved, to be at peace – yet we fall short. We never have enough money, time, etc. - you can fill in the blanks. On top of that, human beings are not always nice and have been doing nasty things to each other for a long time. Why? What is it that turns a person from love to hate, from kindness to cruelty, from goodness to evil? Why are we destined to suffer – even when we do our best to avoid it?"

The Catholic teachings about Original Sin had haunted me since my childhood, and it was this doctrine I hated the most. All my life, I felt as if I could never get away from the idea that I would be trapped in sin forever, no matter what I did. I stood guilty and condemned. As I reflected back on my years outside the Church, I realized that I had never managed to free myself from those feelings of guilt, and I was still running from them.

"So why do we suffer and inflict suffering?" I wanted to know. Our priest answered, "Understanding 'The Fall', and our relationship to Original Sin, is the key to beginning to understand why there is suffering in the world." He explained that the Eastern Orthodox understanding of Original Sin and its consequences differed in important respects from the Roman Catholic teaching.

That was as far as he went with me that day — as a wise teacher, my priest only gave me as much information as I could digest at once. But as time went on, I discussed many other issues with him. My questions came one after the other: Why are only men allowed to be priests? What options do women have in the Eastern Church? Is Christ really God and man? What about evolution and reincarnation?

"These issues are matters that you need to read about and resolve within your heart and soul," he'd say. "I and others are here to support you, but you need to do your homework and pray about these matters." I appreciated this approach, even though I was often left with more questions than answers. Not one person tried to convince me. Instead, they supported me to explore the Orthodox faith with my conscience as my guide. By summer, I had worked through my most intense reactions to the Church and Christianity.

Despite my new openness and inquisitiveness, however, I still lacked the same spiritual desire and hunger that I witnessed in Greg. My husband pursued his newly found religion with great devotion and love. I was confronted and challenged by his commitment – his inner fervor contrasted with my lack of spiritual zeal. Why wasn't I engaged in the same way as Greg? I didn't know the answer. After all, I had lost much of my old defensiveness and hostility for Christianity. I liked the parish, the people and our priest. I had even started doing morning prayers with Greg, singing with the choir and getting to know people in our church. I was motivated to do these things because it was important to Greg, however, not because I had any great desire of my own to grow towards God in the Church. Ultimately, wanting to be with Greg was not enough to keep me going to church on a regular basis.

After much deliberation, I decided that I would only attend church on special occasions, like Christmas. I felt I was not truly cut out to be a Christian and besides, I had important things to do. I had started working six days a week to accommodate the amount of work required to prepare for our organization to go to Auschwitz. Overworked and overtired, I began to feel spiritually disconnected. When I meditated, I would only hear a lonely silence. Only in my classes did I find some solace, when I led others in our guided meditations. Although I loved to travel, I was anxious about our upcoming trip. When I boarded the plane for Auschwitz, part of me was absolutely terrified.

Good and evil exist, and not just as abstract principles. Although being sexually abused, and encountering human suffering in India had taught me something about the nature of evil, my trip to Auschwitz taught me more about these matters in a very powerful way. Going to Auschwitz forever changed the way I viewed good and evil; going to Auschwitz forever changed my life and my soul.

Chapter 3

Auschwitz
"The Turning Point"

It was 1995, and the 50th anniversary of the liberation of Auschwitz. Claire wanted to honor the memory of her father and those who had suffered and died there during the Holocaust. She wanted to bring people to Auschwitz to witness and to begin a discussion about how to create a peaceful world. She wanted Jews and Gentiles to make this journey together. Her vision was so compelling that even those of us who didn't have a clue as to what we would experience there were willing to put everything we had into making her dream a reality. We had all worked six days a week for six months to prepare.

At Auschwitz, we hosted three seminars over twelve days. I participated in two of them. We called our workshops in Auschwitz *The Turning Point,* and for our promotional materials, we used a black and white photograph of sunlight shining through the trees at a turn in the road. Claire had asked the question ahead of time, "How is your journey to Auschwitz going to become your personal 'Turning Point'?" We managed to gather three hundred individuals together from many backgrounds, including Jews, Palestinians, Bosnians, Europeans and Americans. As workshop participants, we took daily walks through the camps and then attended workshop sessions in the late afternoons and evenings. Six survivors of Auschwitz escorted us: five Jews, one of whom was a woman, and a Christian man who had been in the French resistance.

Auschwitz was the largest death camp created by the Nazis. An average of 100,000 prisoners were housed and enslaved in it at any given time. There is now a museum in the first and smaller part of Auschwitz, *Auschwitz 1*, which was originally a training camp for Polish soldiers. On our first day, we toured the museum. The first displays dealt with the beginning of the Holocaust and depicted how the roots of genocide deepened over time. As you progress through the museum, you see how skillfully propaganda was used by Hitler and his henchmen to capitalize on the fears and anger of the German people and direct that hostility towards Jews, as well as other minorities.

In the next section of the museum, we arrived at a series of rectangular rooms filled with huge mounds of shaved hair and thousands of shoes and suitcases taken from the prisoners. We then walked through the wretched living spaces where prisoners had been barracked. We passed a bloodstained wall where executions happened on a daily basis. I felt increasingly distraught as we continued on. The end of the tour brought us to the only intact small gas chamber remaining in Auschwitz – all the other gas chambers had been blown up by the Germans before the Allied troops arrived. When I approached the door of the gas chamber, I almost collapsed under the weight of emotion and horror and I burst into tears. Nauseated, I staggered into the gas chamber where the sense of suffering and the anguish of countless souls were still palpable in the atmosphere.

How could human beings do such things to each other? This was only my first day of witnessing such evil and I was not sure I could endure more, but we soldiered on. Our subsequent days were spent in *Auschwitz 2*, the wicked mother of all concentration camps. *Auschwitz 2* was so enormous that one could not perceive an end to it. We entered under its archway of hell and went straight to the train tracks where prisoners arrived. Within minutes of disembarking, guards divided the prisoners into those that would live and those that would die. Our guide, Bernard, said farewell to his mother and sister on those tracks. They went one way; he and his father went the other.

From there, we went to the blown up remains of multiple gas chambers that were as large as a football field and had the capacity to kill 20,000 people a day. Thousands more were killed in other areas of the camp in mass graves. An unnatural quiet haunted Auschwitz where the mass exterminations had been conducted - not one bird was to be seen or heard in the areas where mass graves and gas chambers once existed. Day after day, we walked and witnessed. A textbook definition of witness is: *one asked to be present at a transaction so as to be able to testify to its having taken place, something serving as evidence or proof.* I felt that each one of us there was being asked to testify, to listen to the unheard voices of those that had suffered and to comfort them.

In our evening sessions after our walks, Claire would ask us, "What are you going to do with what you have witnessed today?" If the suffering and deaths of all these people are not to be in vain, if we do not want history to repeat itself, what could we do to create a 'Turning Point' in our lives and the lives of others? I struggled to find my answers to these questions. Walking through the camps, I had one of the most sobering realizations of my life: evil is not something vague or imaginary. Having witnessed the unspeakable horrors that occurred at Auschwitz, I desperately wanted, with all my heart, to be someone who upheld goodness in the world. As far as I knew, this was the only way I could combat such evil.

I had come to Auschwitz feeling confused, struggling, disconnected and depressed. After I arrived in Auschwitz, I realized that my troubles were so small compared to the tragedy and evil I witnessed there. After a workshop, I would generally leave with a plan for accomplishing the changes I wanted to make in my life. I would then create concrete steps and timelines to achieve those goals. But when I returned home, I wasn't able to integrate the experience of Auschwitz into any plan or list of goals. All the tools I previously utilized seemed useless, and none of my usual spiritual techniques and meditations for calming my mind and heart brought relief. Instead, after my meditations or personal channeling, I'd feel more disturbed and agitated. My distrust of others and displaced anger grew worse as each day passed. My commitment to uphold the "goodness in the world" faded away, as if it had been just a dream.

I couldn't talk about my reactions to Auschwitz with anyone. Wasn't I supposed to be the one in charge, the group leader and the brilliant channel who knew just what she was doing, what she was listening to and where she was going? Four months after Auschwitz, I felt as if I were on the verge of a nervous breakdown. One day, I could no longer tolerate the onslaught of negative thoughts and desires that assailed me. In my spiritual battle, I knew I was losing. "Forget about saving the world," I thought. "I can't even save myself from me!" I rolled up in a ball under the covers of our bed, sobbing and moaning. At this moment, my husband walked in the door. He had watched me decline over the last few months, and had felt the same sorrow and powerlessness I had felt when he had been so lost. When he came towards me, I crawled out of bed and on my hands and knees, I laid my head on Greg's feet and asked him for help.

Chapter 4

I Reach the Center of My Labyrinth

Greg held me while I continued to weep. He stroked my hair and comforted me until I finally calmed down. Then he said, "Okay, I want to help you, but I fear you're not going to like what I have to say".

"Go ahead," I sniffed. "I'll listen now. What I'm listening to in my head is destroying me, and I fear it will destroy all that I hold precious. I see in you what I do not have in myself. You have inner peace. Please help me."

My dear husband replied, "Forgive me for saying this, but you are spiritually arrogant and do not know the first thing about prayer or how to be in a real relationship with God. I can only say this to you based on my own experience of the cost of my form of arrogance. You need humility, prayer and Christ to get you out of the mess you're in. You know I've been where you are now." His words went straight to my heart. In his own kind way, my husband was saying I was a spiritually arrogant hypocrite! I had built a very good case maintaining that priests, nuns and others were hypocrites… but, me?

For years, I had felt hard-hearted towards Christ like the Jewish elders and people of Christ's time. His presence sent shock waves through the Jewish community. Even though they'd been waiting for the promised Messiah, they wanted Him to liberate them from the Romans and from oppression at the hands of other nations. Many expected a worldly warrior king. Yet Christ said that He and those that seek to follow Him are not of this fallen world (*John 16: 18-19*). He came to free people from their egos and negative passions, not to take on the current political establishment, which was a deep disappointment to those seeking a worldly liberator.

I, too, had been seeking liberation from my worldly suffering. Bitter and angry, disappointed with the Church, I grew to hate what I had loved as a child. I turned away from Christ and the Church to the New Age and Eastern Religions. In a moment of truth, I had to admit Greg was right – I *was* spiritually arrogant and a hypocrite. What I witnessed in Auschwitz caused me to doubt my New Age beliefs. My eyes were newly opened to the essential value of Christian teachings on good and evil.

Greg continued, "How can you claim to be 'spiritual' while negating the importance of God?"

"What do you mean?" I said. "I believe in God!"

Greg continued, "You believe in God when it's convenient for you and on your terms, but you have a rather one-sided relationship. You want to have your cake and eat it, too. How can you have time to be with God when you spend all your time talking and praying to your "guides and ascended masters"? Do you truly know who you are praying with and to?"

Greg went on, "Based on your state of mind lately, would you finally be willing to reconsider the possibility that you're being misled in your meditations and thoughts?"

How many times over the last few years had Greg tried to have this conversation with me? How did I always respond? I'd get angry and defensive. Me misled? How could I, a master channel, who had foolproof methods for screening out demonic forces, be misled? I was right and he was wrong. How could he think that what I was doing was not good for me? Such grief I caused him!

Yet, out of my suffering the last few months, I was finally able to hear what he was saying. Although I didn't want to admit it publicly, I had been asking myself the same question from time to time. Could I truly be listening to the wrong voices? I decided to test the theory. Right then and there, I prayed an exorcism prayer, "In the name of Jesus Christ, Satan be gone." To my utter shock, I saw a small red devil by my right shoulder, horns, tail and all, run away! Horrified, I screamed and told Greg what I had just seen.

Greg replied, "Perhaps now you might consider what I have been saying? Perhaps you're experiencing a form of demonic attack?" I started feeling dizzy and sick. I thought back to Auschwitz, where I had witnessed the cost and consequences of following a false ideology. In a flash of insight, I saw the connection between the evil of Auschwitz and my activities. Had I delved too deeply into the occult?

I could no longer be casual about good or evil. I was being asked to choose. In reality, my conscience had been pleading with me for months to wake up to the contradictions and denials of my life.

I needed God! The longing for Him had always been present in my seeking, but on this day, I woke up. My turning point meant choosing to believe in the goodness of God and choosing to commune with Him. I had to begin to learn how to distinguish good from evil, true from false. Greg asked me, "Perhaps you're lacking the proper tools to truly discern evil from good?" I had to admit, with some relief, that he was right. I had arrived at the center of my labyrinth; the "something missing" was actually a *Someone*.

No wonder my meditations stopped working for me! No wonder I felt as though I were in a void following my departure from church! I needed to experience what my life would be like if I continued living it my way—hell, the absence of God's presence. I was now ready to let God back in. A small portion of my hardened heart was finally breaking open.

That afternoon I picked up my Orthodox prayer book again and started reading prayers with Greg. Greg was on target: for all my spiritual knowledge, I knew little about prayer. "This is where the path to having a real relationship with God and learning true discernment begins," Greg stated, handing me a tiny little book called *The Path of Prayer*.[5]

The author wrote in the Preface, "Prayer for so many of us in the West is one dimensional and incomplete." I could relate to that sentence only too well, since I had turned to Eastern meditation to escape Catholic prayers. Yet, this writer said that prayer could be holy and profound, and that through prayer, the soul could be filled with grace and love and the tangible presence of the Holy Spirit. At that moment, I began to understand that prayer, like a flowing liquid, can not be grasped or put on display. Veneration and contemplation meant so much more than simply asking for things.

After reading *A Path of Prayer* and chanting the prayers for three months, morning and evening, a wonderful thing happened. I felt a longing in my heart to go to back to church again. This time I knew I was returning so that I could be with God.

Chapter 5

Oh no! Am I becoming one of them?

"Will I become *one of them?*" It didn't take long for my fears and reactions to kick in as I began to embrace the practices of Orthodox Christianity. I was tormented by the thought that I was becoming *one of them.* I also feared that my non-Christian friends would have the same thought. Some of them did. Why couldn't the door of my spiritual awakening, which had closed when I was a child, be re-opened somewhere other than into the Christian realm?

While dealing with other people's reactions and doubts as well as my own, I noticed that thanks to my last few months of prayer, I was no longer feeling empty, but gratefully humbled.[6] I use the word grateful because I was managing to stay spiritually afloat in a stormy sea of change. It was humbling because I knew I couldn't take credit for my return to sanity. Since humility is the opposite of spiritual arrogance or pride, I realized that what I was experiencing was a good thing. I reflected on how thinking highly of one's self is so valued and encouraged in our society. The rich and famous are everywhere and some of us make a study of their lifestyles. Until just a few months ago, I had thought quite highly of my spiritual accomplishments and myself. Yet, for all I had learned, I was realizing now how little I knew about how to acquire perfect love and trust in God.

What if I didn't need to spend my life trying to prove that I was perfect or better than others and then falling into a sense of failure and depression when I didn't succeed? What if God's grace could transform me? What if I could learn how to turn my mind, heart, and will towards God through prayer? What if I could learn how to live a life based on acquiring virtue, instead of seeking the hidden secrets of the universe? What if I learned to be meek and pure of heart, rather than spiritually arrogant and proud?

I perceived that fulfilling these 'what ifs' would allow me to keep the commitment I made in Auschwitz to support goodness in the world. Perhaps becoming "one of them'" might be worth whatever the cost might be? Clearly, I was attached to other people's approval of me and I didn't like to be seen as a failure in the eyes of my friends. If I became a practicing Christian, many of my peers would view this change as a repudiation of what I had believed and taught for years. A part of me liked being in charge and fighting *my way* out of my struggles. I was proud of my intellect and its ability to delve into occult teachings, which I believed placed me into an intellectual hierarchy. Entering into Eastern Orthodox Christianity seemed to be the exact opposite of where I had resided intellectually and spiritually for almost thirty years.

My husband and others in my church would talk about spiritual warfare. "What is that?" I asked.

"A battle for your soul is being fought on unseen levels," my husband explained. "It was the providence of God that revealed the devil to you several months ago. Without seeing that little red devil, you would not have believed me when I said you were being spiritually attacked by demonic forces."

"You're right. I wasn't even aware that there was a battle for my soul taking place." I sighed. "If I hadn't started praying and going to church, I fear I would have lost my mind. But I don't have a clue as to what will happen to my work or my life as a result of the changes I'm starting to make."

I had continued my private practice as a spiritual counselor despite all my inner conflicts. This may seem hard for Christian readers to understand, but I didn't feel compelled to walk away from my work. Rather, I felt truly inspired for the first time in several years. I wanted to bring what I was discovering to my students and clients. They could see that I had made an internal shift, but what did that shift mean for them? How were my choices going to affect them in our classes and sessions?

For starters, I chose to utilize the reactions of my students to my Orthodox Christian journey as a starting point for conversation. Many students had been like me, harboring animosity towards God and religion. I invited my students to use our work as an opportunity for healing. Instead of our usual guided meditations, I began to talk about the value and benefits of prayer. I would read aloud beautiful prayers to God from a variety of sources, followed by peaceful contemplation on the Divine. This seemed tolerable to all my students and supportive of my journey. At the same time, I stopped invoking spirit guides or ascended masters, since I was now unclear as to who and what they might truly be. "Courage, Polly, courage!" I would say to myself, as I forged ahead into unknown and uncomfortable territory.

Not one person in our little church or the larger Orthodox community pressured me about anything during this transition. They could see that I was wrestling with my beliefs, philosophies and years of spiritual training, which frequently seemed diametrically opposed to Eastern Orthodox principles. My mind and spirit hungered for the peace I experienced during Orthodox prayers and church services, yet I was still plagued by doubts.

I remembered the intimacy I had felt with God on shamanic journeys. I then recalled the hope I felt on my last journey. God had promised me that I would find the way to be intimate with Him without the assistance of shamanic medicine. Had I found the way? What about my beliefs in reincarnation, channeling and all the different spiritual teachings I had studied? How could I know if Eastern Orthodox Christianity was truly the right path for me? Choosing to go deeper required such a leap of faith; I needed an undeniable sign from God that I was, indeed, on the right track.

I shared my concerns with Greg and he suggested that I call Fr. Simeon, the priest who had been with Greg the day prior to the healing of his hand. "Fr. Simeon came from a somewhat similar metaphysical background", Greg offered. "Perhaps he could help you as well?" So, I called him and arranged a time for us to converse by phone.

In our first conversation, Fr. Simeon and I shared our backgrounds with each other. I empathized with his descriptions of his childhood struggles and his life as a former spiritual healer. Once we had established this common ground between us, he questioned me more deeply about my fears in our next conversation. I expressed my need to know if this time, I was truly choosing what God wanted. Fr. Simeon responded, "To enter into a real relationship with God, one based on trust, requires having faith, believing in the goodness of God and being open to the teachings of the Church. You can have doubts, but you cannot allow your reactions to pull you away from God this time. For then you will fall into mistrust again, as you have in the past. Are you willing to trust in God?"

I felt a struggle starting to rise up in me after Fr. Simeon asked me this question. I hesitated. Then I thought, "My struggle right now is about commitment. Fr. Simeon is asking me to make a commitment to trust God. He is asking me to choose to believe that God is good even when I'm afraid or in doubt."

I took a deep breath and said, "Yes, I'm ready to trust in God."

Suddenly my heart became warm – then hot! The warmth then moved through my entire body! I burst into tears, for I suddenly remembered what had happened years ago. "This warmth is the same warmth that embraced me as a child in the chapel at the convent!" I exclaimed. Fr. Simeon replied, "The warmth in your heart is the Holy Spirit moving within you. God has given you your sign." The following Sunday, when I reached the prayer corner in our chapel devoted to Mary, I fell on my knees – again crying – for the sweet presence of the Mother of God I had felt as a child was with me again! Fr. Simeon was right – I had my sign.

This time the warmth did not cool as it had when I was a child. When I became overwhelmed with doubts and fears, I would start praying to God, asking Him to help me to see what was true and good, and then warmth would fill my heart. [7] *"Indeed, a most wonderful thing"* was starting to grow in me.

In my years of seeking companionship with my guru, lama and guides, I always attempted to create intimacy with divinity through intermediaries. At the time, they seemed authentic enough. Yet I still thirsted. Why? My search for deep communion with God had now brought me to the realization that what I was seeking could be found in the practice of Eastern Orthodox Christianity. No human being could have arranged the providential turns in my labyrinth that lead me to this realization. Only God could have laid out the path that led me back to Him. I felt humbled and in a state of awe. Reluctantly but gratefully, I was becoming one of them!

Chapter 6

Walking a Narrow Path

My unrealistic notions of, "what the right path would look like when I found it…" disappeared as I began stumbling along what the Holy Fathers of the Church call 'The Narrow Path' of the Orthodox faith. Thoughts constantly bombarded me and my emotions frequently blocked the way. I felt as if there was no safety net below me and I was carrying so much baggage that I needed to discard. Clearly, the only way to move forward was to let go.

Seeing a demonic manifestation certainly convinced me I was in a spiritual battle, but I still had so much to learn before I could understand the warfare that results when a soul turns from occultist practices towards the living God. Dare I compare my experiences to that of the struggle between good and evil in *The Lord of the Rings*? I could relate to Frodo in the dark of Mordor with the Light of Galadriel in his hand. I felt a faintness of heart similar to that which he experienced on the perilous journey he had undertaken for the sake of others. Frodo wanted goodness to triumph and so did I. Forces visible and invisible constantly exerted pressure on Frodo to quit. How I struggled to surmount my doubts and fears – to stay with the warmth in my heart – my Light of Galadriel in the darkness.

Leaving the world I knew, I continued my inward journey - my New Age, metaphysical beliefs now clashing openly with my newfound

Orthodox beliefs. I would go to my classes and teach others, all the while wondering, "What is going to happen to all that I have studied and created? Why am I being called to Eastern Orthodox Christianity? Couldn't I find some peace of mind and heart in something more acceptable to others?" I would lament to God. Alas, to the utter dismay of my ego, but to the rejoicing of my spirit, the only moments I found inner peace and stillness were when I prayed alone or was in church.

God bless my husband, who endured the brunt of my dismay and struggles. As Frodo had Sam to help him on his perilous journey, I had Greg. One day my husband asked me, "Would you like to visit St. Paisius Orthodox Monastery with me tonight? There is an interesting lecture after prayers and dinner, and I think you'd experience a taste of the deeper spiritual life that is possible within the Orthodox Church."

"Do you really think I'm ready?" I asked. "Yes, I do," Greg answered with a smile. "A visit to the monastery is exactly what you need. I want you to become more aware of the nature of the spiritual battle you're fighting. Monasteries are the best place to learn how to more properly arm yourself for spiritual battle."

"At this point," I said with a sigh, "anything that would help me gain a better footing on my precarious path would be helpful!"

Since the inception of my inner quest for enlightenment, I always felt hopeful before visiting a monastery or ashram, despite being ultimately disappointed with both my Hindu ashram and Tibetan monastery experiences. My first spiritual awakening occurred in a Catholic women's monastery, and since St. Paisius was also a women's monastery, I was once again filled with hope and anticipation as we set out on our pilgrimage.

From our home in Tiburon, the monastery was more than an hour's drive. We were about halfway there when I began to feel extremely uncomfortable in my body. An intense burning and agitation struck me in my lower abdominal areas and down my legs. With each mile my discomfort increased. I started squirming in my seat and groaning.

"What is the matter with you, Polly?" Greg asked.

"I feel so uncomfortable," I cried. "I have this intense sensation raging within me that burns. I want to crawl out of my skin. I feel as if I am a caged tiger crashing my body against the bars of my cage to escape a fire that's enveloping me. I'm in agony!"

Greg didn't know what to make of this. "Do you want me to turn around and go home?" he asked. "No," I emphatically replied. "I think what I'm feeling is related to going to the monastery. Keep going!" Greg suggested I start praying, so I did, and he joined in. I clung to our prayers to help me endure the discomfort until we arrived. When our car entered the gateway of the monastery, the sensations stopped.

"How are you?" Greg asked. "Better, thank God!" I said, immensely relieved. "Let's go in and see what happens. Hopefully, this was a one-time event." Stepping out of the car, I shyly approached some of the people gathered outside the chapel who were awaiting the bell which called worshippers to prayer. Greg started to introduce me. "Oh, you're Greg's wife! We've heard so much about you from Greg! It's so wonderful you could finally visit us!" one of the nuns exclaimed, barely letting him finish.

"Yes, I'm glad I could be here at last, too! Greg has shared so much with me about his love for your monastery!" I replied.

The nuns wore black, the monastic symbol of death for the world, and their bodies were covered up from head to toe in a style similar to that worn by the nuns from my Catholic childhood. Unlike the world outside, within the shelter of the monastery one does not want to draw attention to oneself, or be a temptation to others. The women pilgrims dressed practically and comfortably, more concerned with modesty than fashion. I had noticed that some of the women in my church preferred more simple attire as well, but being my mother's daughter, I dressed stylishly, conscious of my "look." Mingling with the other women at the monastery, I began to appreciate their modest attire. For standing throughout the long worship services, the comfortable clothing and shoes made practical sense and were less of a distraction to other worshippers.

The lovely, rustic chapel at St. Paisius was nestled in the shade of Redwoods at the bottom of a mountain glade. Beautiful icons of the saints adorned the wooden walls and glowed from the reflected candlelight. Incense filled the air. Men stood on one side of the chapel, women on the other. The angelic nuns' voices contrasted with the hearty, rougher voices of the men throughout the vigil service. After our service, we proceeded to the trapeza (dining room in monastic terminology) for the communal meal; again, women sat on one side, men on the other.

We also didn't speak during dinner, but listened instead to selected spiritual readings. Their hospitality and gentle manners disarmed me. After a short break, the lecture started. By the end of the evening, my feet were aching and my body was shivering—I had not dressed properly for the occasion or for the early April weather.

On the way home in the car, Greg asked, "How are you feeling now?"

"Well, aside from frozen and sore, okay. I didn't have any kind of earth-shattering experience, but I didn't experience any adverse reactions either." I paused. "The people were quite welcoming and I felt safe," I concluded.

"Do you want to return?" Greg asked.

"Yes," I answered. "But next time, I won't dress to impress anyone – I'll dress for warmth and practicality. My feet were killing me in the shoes I wore. I noticed many of the women wore sneakers. And by the way, why are all the mirrors in the bathrooms covered up?"

"That's to help us take our focus off ourselves," Greg explained. "It takes some time to get used to the simplicity of the dress and the monastery etiquette."

"Simplicity is a good word to describe my overall experience," I mused. "Even the food was prepared in a simple, healthy way - not for pleasure but for sustenance. I'm still digesting the experience, no pun intended!"

Much to my dismay, on the next several occasions when we visited St. Paisius Abbey, I again experienced the burning sensations as we drew nearer to the monastery, only with greater intensity! On my fourth visit, I mustered up the courage to ask for help when we arrived. I approached the father confessor of the monastery and one of the elder nuns and asked for a private consultation regarding my physical discomfort. They listened attentively and then asked me specific questions about my past, especially related to my sexuality. Slowly and tearfully, I divulged the unhappy details of my sexual past: the initial abuse I had endured as a child, the sexual nightmares that plagued me during my teens, my marital indiscretions, my promiscuous behavior between my marriages and the various spiritual initiations I had experienced, some of which had opened up my desires and lusts. I also disclosed my profession as a channel and spiritual teacher to them.

"Well, that is quite a history and story!" exclaimed the priest, a Jewish convert from New York. "Maybe we should bring out some garlic and holy water!"

"Thanks for putting me at ease!" I laughed, grateful for his humor.

"In all seriousness," he continued on, "the kinds of sensations you experience on the way to our monastery are often related to sexual abuse or the lack of discretion in one's past. There is a wonderful story we read during Lent called the *Life of St. Mary of Egypt*.⁸ St. Mary was a prostitute, who with the miraculous assistance of the Mother of God, vowed to change her life. She left the world and became an ascetic in the Egyptian desert. She lived alone there for many years until she encountered a hieromonk (a priest who is also a monk). She shared her story with Abba Zosimas. It is quite remarkable and worth reading, especially given your past. St. Mary related how she had fought for years to overcome burning sensations and other temptations that would grip her."

The priest explained further, "Sexual violation is a state of intrusion that marks one's soul through the body. It is as if the demonic realm has a portal through which it can enter into one's body after the violation. This rip in your soul's fabric can heal, but healing requires prayer, fasting and deep internal repentance, for the very being of your soul was damaged when you were abused.

"We think perhaps your struggle on the way to our monastery was, at least in part, the reaction of demonic forces to the approaching Light of the monastery. Demonic forces can sense the impending confrontation with Christ. You were right to continue to come here despite your discomfort, for healing lies within the Church for such things. The closer you strive to come to God, the more intense the demonic realm strives to derail you. There are unseen battles being fought on many levels as one strives to live a godly life."

The priest then blessed me. The sister gave me a hug and both of them said that they would pray for me. Throughout our conversation, I felt quite a bit of activity in the same areas of my body, and I felt quite uncomfortable in a different way, difficult to describe. It was as if our conversation had swept my internal house clean of unwanted visitors. I felt relieved to have confessed my sexual sins, and my newly opened eyes could see the battle for my soul being waged within my own body!

The priest and nun cautioned me as we walked back to their chapel, "You're not finished with the attacks and temptations. Now that we have rousted this layer of demonic troublemakers, these forces will seek other ways to undermine your path to God."

I shared everything with Greg on the way home in our car. "Do you think I actually had demons attached to me? Is that not demonic possession in some form?" I asked Greg.

"Well, I'm certainly no expert in this field, but I believe that in the process of channeling, you opened yourself up to what you thought were 'good guides'". As Greg talked, I recalled numerous occasions when I had been greeted with an invitation from a new "being of light" to work with me and my students. I had considered it an honor at the time.

"There was one entity in particular that swirled around me and then entered my body – it was gold in appearance", I related. "I remember that I felt the impact of its entry. I was stunned for several days afterward."

"This has been my concern for you ever since I returned to Christianity," Greg said gently. "It's so easy for demons to disguise themselves. That's why the saints themselves refuse any such advances by so-called 'angelic beings' that try to flatter their egos. You felt flattered, did you not?"

"Yes, I did," I admitted.

Greg continued, "That was how they seduced you, through what the Church teachers call vainglory. Demons once were angels of the light. The saints of the Church say that one third of the heavenly angels fell with Lucifer when he tried to overthrow God. These fallen angels live in the air, which is why channeling is so dangerous. They can read our thoughts and use them to turn us against each other and away from goodness and God. It's amazing how we can see demons in a movie, yet somehow think they're not real."

I pondered all of these things in my heart as we drove home. Thankfully, after this visit, the sensations did not return again.

Chapter 7
Temptations

It was now late spring. Thanks to my visits to the monastery, I felt as if I had a better footing on my precarious path. Gradually adjusting to the Orthodox customs and services, I felt more at home in church and more at ease with the other worshippers. I was also learning more about the dogmatic theology and basic beliefs of the Church. Although the clergy at the monastery had warned me that I wasn't finished with the attacks and temptations, I lacked the spiritual discernment to understand what this meant, and I began to feel more comfortable.

The admonitions of my monastic friends faded from my memory. At first, I didn't notice the new temptation that began eating away at me. Even before our trip to Auschwitz, sensitive issues and situations had arisen relating to my work partnership with Sam and Claire. Unable to confront them or address these festering issues, I began to allow judgmental, blameful thoughts to creep into my mind. I flirted with the temptation to shirk my responsibilities in our partnership. As a result of the confinement of my narrow spiritual search of the last several months and my heavy schedule of work and duties, I felt burned out and fettered - like a horse that was bridled and unable to run freely. I wanted freedom!

Out of force of habit, I chose the route most familiar to me - I unfortunately chose to blame and judge other people, yet again. I also was aware that other individuals in the U.S. agreed with some of my judgments and I started a rebellion. Isn't that how one gains freedom – by revolution? I was attending church, but was listening to my questionable guidance again. I should have sensed that something was wrong with my approach, for I was often sick to my stomach and had a bad taste in my mouth that wouldn't go away. I felt angry and was having difficulty praying; in spite of these red flags, however, I continued my destructive behavior, disregarding the little voice in the background that was trying to warn me.

"Never trust your own thoughts," the monks had cautioned me. I had heard this valuable advice several times at the monastery, but I still didn't apply it to myself. Why would I? After all, I was a trained channel - people came to *me* for advice. Surely, I could trust my own thoughts.

During our summer seminar, I began to see how far I had strayed from my path. My internal Auschwitz had struck again! I felt shock and dismay as the seminar process forced me to take a hard look at myself once again. I wept bitter tears over the next several days and apologized to many of my co-workers. Then I finally uttered the words I had feared to say for years.

"I need to resign my position. I need to trust that together we will find a way to make my departure work for everyone." I heaved a sigh of relief - the world did not fall apart when I uttered those words! "I'm not clear what my role in our organization will be in the future, but we need to find a way to transition other people into my position. I need time to redefine my life and goals." Sam and Claire reluctantly agreed, for they could see that change was in the wind and healthy for all concerned.

We designed a plan that would take a full year to accomplish, in part because staff needed to be brought over from France to replace me. I felt God's protection throughout that year, while I struggled back onto solid spiritual footing, and I was able to responsibly transition out of my key position.

I continued to reflect about how easily I could fall off my narrow path to God if I allowed myself the illusion that I was in control. "When will you get it, Polly?" I asked myself soberly. "When? What is it going to take next time? Will a car crash stop you? What is it going to take? Who will you damage along the way next time? Wake up! You don't have the discernment or spiritual skill to stop yourself. You're on your ninth life! This is it!"

The reality of my predicament overwhelmed me; without God, I could, and would, self-destruct. Yet God had mercifully spared me from the worst consequences of my actions. Why was I spared? Why did God mercifully stand between me and my bad choices? I suddenly realized the answer: God loved me. He had let me fall just far enough, in the hopes that I'd wake up to my need for Him. It was up to me—I had to be the one to choose to live my life differently. I determined I would never allow myself to behave in such an ego-driven manner again.

That's how my summer of 1996 came to an end. I had truly reached the center of my labyrinth and was now walking out of it, into the beginning of a real relationship with God. For the first time in my life, I understood that struggles would be part of my life until my last breath. If I wanted a real relationship with God, I'd have to begin by taking responsibility for my fallen state. The only way I'd be able to gain control over my ego was to surrender it to God. If I could learn to love and become one with God, and place Him at the center of the universe rather than my own selfish ego, I could become trustworthy and perhaps of some use to others. I could live differently with whatever struggles and suffering would be part of my life, if my life included a life in and with God.

I had attempted to quench my spiritual thirst through countless paths – only to thirst and hunger more deeply than before. Tired of wandering from one place to another to find rest, I wanted a spiritual home and I knew now where to go. With all my heart and soul, I longed to receive the mystical sacraments of the Eastern Orthodox Church. I was ready to convert.

Part III

My Conversion

Chapter 1

What is Conversion? Who is God?

I had literally and spiritually journeyed to many faraway countries. I had spent years thinking terrible thoughts about God, the Catholic Church and Christians. Like the prodigal son,[9] I had disowned and rejected my heavenly Father. Because I was beginning to relate to God now as a Person, I could see how I had wounded Him, and others too, by my behavior. Clearly, I needed to crush my pride, humble myself before God, confess what I had done and place all my hope in His mercy and forgiveness. On bended knees, with pain in my heart, I was returning home.

Normally, new converts are received into the Church on two specific holy days, either Theophany (the feast commemorating Christ's baptism by John in the Jordan River), or Holy Saturday on Easter weekend. My husband, Fr. Chris and our church community were so relieved that I was finally ready to take the plunge that they all agreed - the sooner the better! Since nothing seemed to happen in the usual way for me (I smile now when I think of this), we set the date for October 13, 1996. Fr. Chris was also moving on to a new assignment and his replacement, Fr. Tom, would arrive soon for the transition. Fr. Chris wanted to preside over my baptism. After all, I was not an easy convert!

My priest gave me two books to read, *Orthodox Dogmatic Theology* and *The Orthodox Church*[10], pertaining to the history, Holy Sacraments and fundamental beliefs of the Orthodox Church. "Your entry back into the Church requires that you agree with Church's teachings," Fr. Chris explained". I want you to especially dwell on what is written in *Orthodox Dogmatic Theology*. As you ponder these chapters, look deep inside yourself. Do you accept and feel aligned with what you are reading? Do our dogmas resonate in you as truth? If not, please come to me and let's talk about what disturbs you. If you cannot be at peace with what is written, we must postpone your baptism."

Again, I felt immense relief. My return to the Church would not be a shoo-in. During this period of preparation, I recalled my last encounter with Becky, years earlier, when my charismatic, evangelical friend had asked me, "Do you accept Jesus as your Savior?"

I still did not feel comfortable saying "yes" to that question. "Is that okay?" I asked Fr. Chris at one point.

"Feeling uncomfortable is a good place for you," he replied. "You already were given to Christ when you were baptized Catholic, but you fell away and disconnected yourself. Now you're in the process of re-choosing your first baptism." My pastor knew all about my anger and suspicions about the Church and Christianity, and he wanted to be sure that my return to the Church was my choice and my responsibility.

I voraciously read *Orthodox Dogmatic Theology* several times, in part because I wasn't able to grasp the deeper meaning of many of the Sacred Mysteries and doctrines the first time around. Amazingly, my spirit resonated with the basic doctrines of the faith. I had come a long way from those car rides when I pounded my hands on the dashboard in my anger towards God and Christianity. I still didn't know how to reconcile my beliefs about reincarnation, my previous spiritual experiences with my guru or my profession as a spiritual teacher with the Church, but Fr. Chris reassured me. "In time, as you progress in Orthodoxy, God will reveal the deeper significance and meaning of His Sacred Mysteries to you. As your mind, heart, body and spirit become healed through God's grace, your questions will be answered one by one."

"What does conversion[11] mean to you?" he then asked me.

"Well, I've witnessed the process of conversion within my husband," I answered. "I've seen the profound shift within Greg that transcends anything he's accomplished spiritually in the past. I watched my depressed husband put his war novels and paint ball games aside and connect with God through his deepening prayer life. The results were astounding!" I continued, "Now I'm starting on my voyage as well. Even if it's only in small increments, my spirit's rudder is changing the direction of my life. I know that learning to trust in God will somehow bring me to safe harbor."

My pastor encouraged me as I studied and prayed my way through the books. "God reveals His mysteries to those who seek to know and love Him – to 'those who hunger and thirst for righteousness'", he said.

"Well, I'm certainly hungry and thirsty for the truth, now!" I exclaimed.

My studies and prayers bore fruit. I remembered my childhood conviction, that God is the source of all that is good. After reading *Orthodox Dogmatic Theology* several times, I came up with my simplified understanding of the unique qualities of the Three Persons of God. The Father is the Source and Creator, the Son is the Word and Manifestation of God's energies in the world, and the Spirit is the Life Force moving and existing in all creation.

Before my return to church, I connected with God through the beauty of nature. On Sunday mornings while my husband was at church, I would go somewhere beautiful. Nature became my cathedral and my sanctuary, a source for healing and for good. In seeking reconciliation with God, the Father, through the created world, I felt this Force which constantly sustains everything, the Source from which all of life flows. When I watched a brilliant sunrise or rays of sunlight streaming through clouds, I began to feel the presence of God the Father within me. This Source did not seem inanimate to me, but alive, unique, intricate and full of personality. I started observing the diversity of people, animals and life on earth; I experienced the energies of God the Father through the unique essence and expression of life in all living things. What peace and inspiration these contemplations brought me.

I then turned my attention to discovering the presence of the third Person of the Holy Trinity, the Holy Spirit. I had often referred to being moved by the Spirit in my classes. What did that mean to me? Where is the Spirit of God? I felt the Holy Spirit when I breathed, when I moved, when I felt the wind on my face. The Breath of Life that God breathed into the first human being was, and is, the Holy Spirit. When I wrote, or felt inspiration in my work, I started to sense the Holy Spirit's presence. "But the fruit of the Spirit is love, joy, peace, longsuffering, gentleness, goodness, faith, meekness, temperance: against such there is no law." (*Gal 5 :22-23*)

My studies had taught me that these virtues, the fruits of the Spirit, quiet the soul and attract the grace of God. With a guileless heart, one can see God and experience being in relationship with God, thus living in the presence of the Holy Spirit. The discipline one practices to refrain from negative passions and thoughts, combined with an active prayer life, deepens one's acquisition of the grace of the Holy Spirit.

Cleansing and purifying one's soul and body in order to attain enlightenment was a discipline I had practiced for years in my Eastern religions. In fact, I'd been a strict vegetarian for twelve years. Yet, this ancient Christian process didn't set forth self-enlightenment or the discovery of an eternal fountain of youth as its goals. The traditions of the Church taught that it would <u>not</u> be through my will that I would acquire the Holy Spirit. Instead, the acquisition of the Holy Spirit would be achieved by God's grace, not because I made it happen through my own efforts. The Church encouraged me to purify my senses and cleanse my mind and body, to prepare a space for God to dwell in me, by practicing virtuous thoughts and actions, prayer, fasting and receiving the Mystical Sacraments of the Church. Ultimately, however, and most importantly, the teachings of the Church and my own destructive tendencies had taught me that I needed the mercy and love of God or all my spiritual efforts would be in vain.

One Orthodox writer described it this way: "The Acquisition of the Holy Spirit is the main aim of man upon this earth, for it is through the ascetic struggle of 'pulling down' the Holy Spirit into a repentant, humble heart that a man gains justification before the face of God. Christ is our Savior only as long as we realize we are perishing: and the acquisition of the Holy Spirit is the actuality of being saved."[12]

In Orthodoxy, our striving is to fast, to pray and to refrain from judgments and other negative passions. These efforts are our starting points for preparation, our part in the gradual conversion of our soul. We withdraw from worldly attachments to indwell with God. We prepare ourselves to receive the Holy Mysteries of the Church in order to commune more deeply with God. I could see that this process of continual conversion would take the whole of my life to accomplish! I worried at times about whether I could turn my will, moment by moment, over to God? That would be a lot of moments! "What about me? What about what I want?" No wonder my pastor insisted that I fully choose and be fully responsible for my re-entry into the Church.

As I bungled along the narrow path to my Father's home, I experienced the comfort of the Holy Spirit. There were times prior to my baptism when I felt sorrowful, lonely or lost - so many areas of my life were changing so quickly. Whereas before I would have turned to my guides, now I turned to God in prayer. Spiritual warmth would envelop my heart at key moments when I needed reassurance. I needed God and He was becoming the source of my consolation. Christ had referred to the Holy Spirit as the Comforter. "And I will pray the Father, and he shall give you another Comforter, that he may abide with you forever; even the Spirit of truth; whom the world cannot receive, because it seeth him not, neither knoweth him: but ye know him; for he dwelleth with you, and shall be in you." (*John 14: 16-17*)

I had read enough Scriptures at this point to know that Christ was the key that would open the door of my Father's house, but I still didn't feel in personal relationship with God the Son, Christ. "The way to the Father is through the Son," said the Gospel. I saw that others felt an intangible, undeniable relationship with and love for Christ. At least I no longer wanted to run away from Him! Would I be able to re-enter the Church without truly knowing Christ? Could I proceed with my baptism? Fr. Chris and my husband reassured me, "You will find what you're seeking. This is one of the mysteries of Christianity that requires a leap of faith and prayer. Your intention is clear. Don't worry. God will answer your prayer and heart's desire in His time."

Chapter 2

The Prodigal Daughter Returns

The eve of my baptism, October 12, 1996, arrived. It was a little over a year since I had returned from Auschwitz. I was attending a Saturday evening vigil service, which is part of Sunday worship in the Eastern Church. The liturgical day begins at sunset, much like it does in the Jewish worship cycle. Our vigil service was several hours long. After attending the service, I would be required to give my life's confession of sins, specific and general, from my childhood up to the present day! Perhaps that's why I could barely stay awake during my baptism eve service—one of those logs I held over my head in EST years ago might have been helpful!

I strained to stay present in prayer and to stand for long periods of time during services. One would think after all my years of meditating and assisting in seminars that I would have perfected the art of staying alert and attentive, but no! I often struggled to subjugate my soul and body during the hours of long services and prayers. My husband and pastor told me that my resistance was part of the spiritual war one needed to fight to regain one's spirit in one's body. "Remember, there are forces at work that do not want you to pray, or return to God outside and inside of you," they reminded me. "The battle for your soul is something you'll fight your whole life." On the eve of my baptism, an epic battle for my life seemed far removed from my floundering soul in its drugged-like stupor. "This is exactly what happened to me in seminars for years!" I thought. "I must be on the right track, but I hate this part of waking up!" My pattern of going unconscious during times of spiritual stress continued during some services – I would recline on several chairs and fall asleep. On other occasions, I couldn't wait for the service to be over. On the eve of my baptism, the thought of revealing the sins of my entire life literally scared me to sleep.

Suddenly, I heard my husband quietly speaking to me, while shaking me awake. "It's time to make your confession," he whispered. I felt very embarrassed! As I approached the priest, my knees were knocking so badly that I almost fell. How many times as a child and teenager had I dreaded going to confession? The notions of being bad and feeling guilty for my perpetual state of sin had dominated my early Catholic experiences. Memories of the priest yelling at me in the confessional as a young girl flashed through my mind again. Although I knew I could trust Fr. Chris, those earlier experiences still haunted me.

I found the Eastern Orthodox teachings about the sacrament of repentance and confession refreshing, and they helped me surmount my fears about the sacrament of confession. Sin is viewed as a sickness of the soul requiring healing, not punishment. Confession is called the Mystery of Repentance.[13] I knew I needed healing and I felt safe with this approach. I was the prodigal daughter returning home. My heavenly Father already knew everything that I had done. I, however, needed to confess everything that had troubled me for years. Standing there next to Fr. Chris, before the icon of Christ, I began the story of my rebellious and wayward life and I started to weep. My priest didn't say anything throughout the entire narrative, other than a few words when I needed encouragement to keep going. After I had finished, I received his blessing and absolution (absolution: "to set free from an obligation or the consequences of guilt") and promptly sat down and continued to cry. My spirit soared with relief. I was no longer afraid of priests and confession. I no longer felt guilty and I was awake!

Chapter 3

My Baptism

Newly baptized Orthodox Christians always receive a baptismal name. Since it's a saint's name, the hope is that the newly illumined will emulate his or her saint's example. My parents named me Paula, my Italian grandmother's middle name. St. Paula was an Italian martyr. Rather than returning to that name, I decided to choose yet another name for myself, perhaps because I longed for this to be a new beginning at every level.

I read about the lives of perhaps a hundred women saints before I read about St. Veronica. Not only was she "the woman with an issue of blood" who touched the hem of Christ's garment and was healed of her blood disorder, she was also the woman who wiped Christ's face as he was carrying the cross to be crucified. Married (unlike most of the saints) and an artist, St. Veronica traveled as a missionary after Christ's death, bringing the word of the gospel of Christ, and the miraculous healing cloth with His image, to others. I identified with her life, especially with regard to her prolonged health struggles and her desire to acquire faith in God.

Several days before my baptism, I shared my intention to assume a new name with my eternally patient parents. Their mouths dropped open. "Not another name change!" they exclaimed, feeling chagrined. "Forgive me!" I assured them. "This is truly the last name change I'll ever make. I've had too many spiritual names given to me in other religions. I need to start fresh. This name will not be my legal name, just my church and communion name." Sighing in relief, they smiled and gave me their blessing to proceed. They were thankful that I was returning to the Church and finding a measure of peace.

The first rays of sunlight appeared on the horizon on my baptismal day. I had hardly slept, spending much of the night reviewing my life and pondering what awaited me. Nervously preparing myself, I chose a twenty-year old, multi-colored cotton outfit that I had bought on my first trip to Hawaii, believing that it symbolized my old life and the many paths I had traveled to find God. With a huge smile on his face, Greg waited for me as I fussed with this and that. "Let's go! You're perfect just the way you are! You don't want to be late, do you?"

My community greeted me with such kindness and love as I entered the church. Fr. Chris prepared me with a blow-by-blow description of what was about to happen. "We're going to recite many prayers, including an exorcism prayer. Then I will ask you to spit three times on the devil."

"Great! I'm ready to spit on Satan!" I enthused. "What trouble he has caused me!"

Father continued, "We'll then proceed to the back yard, where I'll anoint you multiple times with holy oil while we recite more prayers. After that, you'll receive your baptism."

"Okay," I said, "I'm ready to take the plunge!"

When the moment of baptism arrived, I stepped up to our baptismal font - an old horse trough filled with semi-warm water - and received my full immersion baptism. While priests don't often re-baptize Christians if they've already been baptized in the Protestant or Roman Catholic faith, I felt the need to be received into the Church again through baptism due to my past involvement with the occult.

Stepping out of the trough, my godparents wrapped several towels around me and I ran upstairs to change into a traditional, white baptismal gown, made for me by a dear friend. I then returned to our chapel to participate in the Divine Liturgy, the Eastern Christian term for Mass. Holding a lit candle with a profound sense of growing joy, I waited to receive the sacraments of chrismation and Holy Communion.

Chrismation is the Orthodox equivalent of confirmation. As I waited for my priest to anoint me with the chrism oil, I remembered my

127

teenage confirmation ceremony. Our class had spent months preparing for the Bishop's visit to our parish. I wasn't at all sure that I wanted to be confirmed in the Catholic Church, but I was doing it because it was expected of me. Studying the doctrines of the Church often made me angry or depressed and increased my sense of unresolved guilt, so I avoided my preparatory studies. During the actual service, I felt numb, terrified that the bishop would call on me to answer a question. My fears were unfounded, however; the ceremony flew by in a blur, its significance disappearing almost immediately from my radar screen. I had been confirmed, but I had not committed to my faith in my heart.

On this October day, however, I was in a completely different frame of mind and heart. During the sacrament of chrismation following my baptism, Fr. Chris anointed me with holy chrism oil. Originally blessed by the Apostles, this holy oil was passed down through Apostolic Succession from the earliest days of Christianity to the present time.

Father anointed my head, eyes, ears, mouth, throat, hands and feet, and then cut off a lock of my hair to give to my godparents[14] for their prayer shrine. With each anointing, the priest sealed me with the grace of the Holy Spirit. I truly felt that I was being protected from spiritual harm - that the portals of my soul, once open to harmful spirits, were now closed and guarded. I could sense a new spiritual strength was starting to abide in me.

Through confession, baptism and chrismation, I was now cleansed, purified and ready to receive the Eucharist, Holy Communion. While prayer and worship services had helped me prepare for my return to the Church, I knew that they were not enough to ensure the spiritual healing I hoped and prayed for, and I yearned for the transformative power of partaking of Holy Communion. During my time of preparation over the past several months, I had watched communicants' eyes become alive with the Holy Spirit after receiving the holy elements. Now at last, I, too, could receive the gift of communion with God.

After receiving the bread and wine, I sat down and wept again. Thirty years had passed since I had left my Father's house. How many spirits had manipulated my soul and body while I wandered in the wilderness? Now I had returned home and evicted all the unwanted troublemakers! What a distance I had traveled to be reunited with the Church. The prodigal daughter had returned.

Chapter 4

A Duck Out of Water

In the first precious days following my baptism, I felt reborn. An undeniable sense of grace and innocence pervaded my days, and I felt pure and light. God had mystically reclaimed me and I saw the world through different eyes, as one "in the world, but not of the world." (Jn 8:23) I felt most comfortable when I was in Church, and the outside world seemed harsh by contrast. A soft, quiet stillness wrapped me in a blanket of peace. I experienced inexplicable joy. Fortunately, I had arranged to take the week off from work after my baptism. I must have sensed that I wouldn't be ready to jump back into my normal routine immediately.

How could this new me relate with others? How could I share with people outside of my church community what was happening inside me? I longed to share my growing relationship with God through Christianity. If I could have brought all my family members and friends into church with me, I would have done so in a heartbeat.

When I emerged from my cocoon a week after my baptism, other people responded to me as I had responded to Becky when she had tried to share the joy of her conversion with me. I should have expected this, but it was difficult nonetheless. I asked myself, "What is it about being Christian that is so different from what I had been before?" Nevertheless, I had changed for good — and there was no going back.

I shifted from offering channeling courses and initiations of the soul to a form of spiritual therapy based on my own struggles to heal my relationship with God. My students were in shock! In the past, I had been able to immediately share any spiritual experience or newfound knowledge with my students, and they looked forward to the next round of teachings that might issue from my channeling and apparent transformations. They had always been open to my guidance and assistance as they aspired to the next spiritual level, and I had been quite successful in marketing the accumulative teachings of my guides.

Even prior to my baptism, I had lost about fifty percent of my long-term students over the course of the year. For them, I was no longer offering something new and exciting. Now that I was addressing the issues one faces when reconciling with God, only those truly seeking Him, rather than another experience, showed interest. Some of my students thought I had regressed, and the hard part was that I understood how they felt, since I had once felt the same way.

Before seeing a demon with my physical eyes, I sincerely believed that I was helping and healing people with the support of beings of light. But after that horrifying vision, I frequently struggled internally about who, and what, I had been open to and working with. Did levels of soul growth exist as I had taught them? What exactly had we been experiencing? Where were we going in my sessions and meditations? These questions haunted me.

Walking in the door to teach my first class after my baptism, I instantly felt like a duck out of water. My students and friends welcomed me back. "How are you?" they queried. "How do you feel? What happened on your big day?" I felt shy and was speechless, a rare state for me! I felt so fragile in my new Christianity. I was no longer "The Expert." I can't even remember what I taught that night. I breathed a sigh of relief when I finished the class and could return home. "God help me! I need to find a middle ground. I have to teach what I believe, and now much of what I had believed, I question. God help me to find the Way and the Truth."

Just how much I had changed internally became apparent several weeks after my baptism, when a New Age colleague invited me to a healing circle for a sick friend. One year prior, this sort of evening would have been an enjoyable experience for me. I felt ill at ease, however, from the moment I walked through the door. Shamans, channels and friends had all gathered for the occasion. Everyone was talking about the newest information that had been channeled by one of the attendees. Being with people who were listening to their guides, and being in a spiritually eclectic setting, increasingly disturbed me the longer I was there. I wanted to leave, but I didn't want to be rude.

At one point, we formed our healing circle around our ailing friend. As the intensity of the energies being channeled increased, I tried to contribute, but I felt so uncomfortable that all I could do was silently recite the Lord's Prayer or a Hail Mary. I wasn't judging my colleagues for what they were doing – I was too busy dealing with my own inner conflicts and was becoming sick to my stomach. I felt peaceful when I arrived. When I left, I felt as though I were covered with green slime! I took a bath and prayed, but I wasn't able to remove this feeling from my being. I continued to feel disturbed until I went to confession a few days later with my new priest, Fr. Tom.

During my confession, I discussed my reactions to the healing circle with Fr. Tom. My reaction was similar to the unease I had felt during the last few years of my first marriage when I had committed marital indiscretions. My new pastor reminded me, "You entered into a monogamous relationship with Christ when you chose to reconcile with the Church. If you pray to anything other than God, it will not sit well with your soul."

Rather than feeling restricted by this admonition, I immediately agreed. "You're right. I never expected to feel so awful in a setting that was so familiar! There *is* a difference between Christianity and other spiritual practices – a big difference, but I hadn't felt that distinction before my baptism. Is this what spiritual discernment feels like?" I asked Fr. Tom, feeling encouraged.

"Yes!" he continued. "Your discomfort is a good sign! The fact that you felt so uncomfortable was good! God's Spirit is alive in you and was objecting to what you were doing! Worshiping or praying to anything other than Christ's authentic Light will disturb you now. You'll feel like a duck out of water."

"That's great!" I exclaimed. "Who would have thought that feeling ill at ease in my spirit, like a duck out of water, would be the first sign that I'm gaining spiritual discernment?" From that time forward, I tactfully declined all similar invitations.

Chapter 5

The Healing Medicine of Eastern Orthodox Christianity

After my baptism, my body, mind, and soul began to heal through the sacraments and teachings of the Church. I had hoped, but not expected this. Each transformation that occurred was an answer to a long-forgotten prayer. In my heart of hearts, I had hoped that I would find answers to my suffering and confusion when I found my true spiritual path; this began to happen beyond my wildest dreams.

My first healing occurred during the annual Pastors' Conference at the monastery in Forestville. Greg and I were so thrilled that we could finally attend a retreat together. Thirty priests and deacons, their families and over fifty lay people gathered for a three-day retreat, which culminated with an all-night vigil and morning Liturgy. "All-night" meant we went to bed around 2 a.m.

I was quite cold when I finally crawled into my sleeping bag after the vigil. My feet felt frozen and my back ached from the physical strain of all our activities. Strangely, this didn't bother me because I felt so spiritually alive. Unlike my baptism, which had been a quiet, indwelling experience, this retreat was a window into the depth of spiritual nourishment available in Orthodoxy. No wonder Greg felt so inspired when he returned from his visits to the monastery. Rather than exhausting me, the all-night vigil filled me with so much energy that I couldn't go to sleep. The hymns we sung echoed in my mind. My heart and body were warm and full of love despite the physical discomfort I was feeling. It dawned on me: I was truly communing with God!

Ten years of searching, struggling and waiting, and here I was, in a most unexpected place, reunited with Him, just as He promised me—without tricks or shamanic medicine. Now, thanks to the spiritual medicine of the Eastern Orthodox Church, I was sober, clear and intimately communing with God. I spent the next few hours immersed in tears as I thanked Him that my narrow path and difficult climb had, indeed, brought me home.

It took my back a week to recover from the retreat but I didn't care—it was worth every ache and pain. I understood now the value of patient endurance while participating in all-night vigils. No wonder people prayed this way!

My second healing came soon thereafter. Greg and I knew that God had brought us together for a spiritual purpose when we first met. Now God was fulfilling that promise and potential as we united in our faith. Having our marriage blessed in the Orthodox Church became the next step in our spiritual journey together.

Our tenth anniversary was approaching. I had been feeling for some time that it would be good to reaffirm our vows in the Orthodox Church. We had both been through so many changes since we eloped and married on December 1, 1986 in Hana, Maui, Hawaii. Our wedding had been quite romantic and fun, in contrast to the ceremony of my first marriage, whose details had been dictated by my former mother-in-law. I had wanted my second wedding ceremony to be free of outside pressure, and Greg had wanted to keep our marriage a secret until after the fact, so eloping seemed the best solution.

That was then. Now, however, we both felt that it was important to restate our marriage vows in church in the presence of our family and friends. We discovered, however, that we were not simply restating our vows; we were being married for the first time, in the eyes of the Church, through the Sacrament of Holy Matrimony. Up until this point, I had been casual in my approach to the event and hadn't even bought a new dress! I woke that Saturday to the realization that I was getting married in Church the next day.

"Hello Polly!" I said to myself. "Are you aware yet that this is a big deal?"

I jumped out of bed and spent the rest of the day shopping, and as I did, I shifted internally. Casual no longer, I started feeling like a nervous bride.

"Greg, are you feeling a little nervous, too?" I asked, when I arrived home with my outfit.

"Yes!" he admitted. "Maybe this is a bigger deal than I thought, too!"

Neither of us slept well that night. The next day, in a profoundly touching service following Sunday Liturgy, Fr. Tom placed crowns on our heads and the choir sang joyful bridal hymns to us. We exchanged vows and rings, and the ceremony culminated with the sharing of wine, multiple blessings from our priest, a procession and the bridal feast.

Greg and I were not prepared for the change that awaited us when we woke the next morning and looked into each other's eyes. "Are you seeing and feeling what I am?" I asked Greg. "Yes!" he whispered. We didn't have to speak what we felt. Neither of us uttered a word. As we gazed into each other's eyes, the window to our souls, we experienced each other as virginal, white, purified and sanctified vessels. How could that be?

For me, this second transformation of the very core of my being and body seemed most miraculous of all. I no longer felt in my soul the trauma of sexual abuse or the residue from my former sexual indiscretions. I felt pure. Could it truly be possible that I had been released from thirty years of pain, and from the violent loss of innocence which I had mourned for so many years? How I had cried out in agony to God during therapy. Now, instead of bitter tears, I was crying for joy with Greg. He said something I will never forget as he gazed into my eyes, "Perhaps we're feeling a little akin to the innocence Adam and Eve felt in Paradise with God before The Fall."

From that moment on, we earnestly prayed that we would cooperate with the grace we'd been given. Receiving the Sacrament of Marriage had transformed both of us.

Chapter 6

"The Fall"

In the days following our marriage in the Church, my studies in the Orthodox faith encouraged me and fulfilled my spiritual hopes and yearnings. To prepare for my baptism, I had studied the teachings of the Orthodox Church relating to The Fall of mankind, as described in Genesis. I had turned my back on the Church, in part, because of my misunderstandings and struggles over the meaning of The Fall and Original Sin. In my 20s, I had happily embraced evolutionary theory, which supported my choice to leave the Catholic Church and the traditional Judeo-Christian teachings about the origins of life and sin. If we had evolved, I didn't need to feel guilty—it was that simple for me then.

By my late 30s, however, I realized that the theory of evolution didn't answer my deeper spiritual questions pertaining to suffering. Why was there so much suffering in the world? Where did suffering come from, if we had evolved from primates? Where do our negative thoughts and actions come from? While preparing for my baptism, I realized that the evolutionary perspective ultimately held no answers to these questions. The Church's teachings, however, on the profound tragedy of mankind's fall from grace, and the loss of our life in Paradise with God, made sense to me. Understanding the personal and collective consequences of The

Fall gave me a new key which helped me clarify my lifelong confusion over suffering's meaning, and my desire to escape it.

I was dumbstruck when I learned, according to renowned saints in the Orthodox Church, that Adam and Eve most likely lasted somewhere between six hours and forty days in Paradise! It occurred to me that I might have lasted for perhaps two minutes in that state of purity. How easily I had taken the virtues of goodness and peace for granted throughout the majority of my life. Perhaps I wasn't so different from Adam and Eve, whose first step towards their loss of grace began with ingratitude?

Then I thought about how much I had struggled with authority, rules and obedience. At least I had that excuse. Adam and Eve were in Paradise. Goodness surrounded them. The only rule God gave Adam and Eve was to not eat of the fruit from the tree in the middle of the garden. This seemed to me to be a fairly simple demand, especially considering the consequences that accompanied God's request. "But of the fruit of the tree which is in the midst of the garden, God hath said, 'Ye shall not eat of it, neither shall ye touch it, lest ye die.'" (Gen 3:3)

Perhaps Adam and Eve were not truly listening to God or taking his words to heart? I had to admit, failing to listen was also one of my frequent faults and because of this, I had often hurt others. Would I have broken that rule if I had known that I would be throwing Paradise away by doing so? Well, I had unknowingly or knowingly thrown away what was precious to me because of self-interest and self-righteousness. I often just needed a little provocation from an outside source. Eve had the suggestions of the serpent, the devil. So, did I – I had even seen him! I, too, had struggled with the desire to possess what was forbidden, with disastrous results.

Then Adam and Eve decided that they wanted to be God. So, did I. They acted on their desires – they disobeyed, lied, blamed each other and then hid from God. So, did I. Adam and Eve didn't repent when God gave them the chance. How often had I *not* properly regretted my actions? Adam and Eve didn't take responsibility for what they had done. My journey was a carbon copy of what I was reading in Genesis, only it was Polly's version, over and over again. When the consequences of Adam and Eve's actions became reality, they lost Paradise.[15] "Adam sat outside of Paradise and wept." St. Silouan developed this theme with haunting poetic beauty: "Adam (who represents all mankind) knew the love and beauty of God, yet cast it aside and in turn cast himself out of the presence of God."[16]

I wept when I realized that I, too, had lost my connection with God and Paradise. How many years had I lived outside of Paradise and the grace of God before my conversion? It had taken me thirty years to change my heart and mind. The morning after our marriage in the Church, I awoke to the awareness that I was, indeed, made in the "image and likeness of God." (Gen. 1:27) I was created by God to dwell in communion and love with Him and others; everything outside of Paradise is what we inherited after The Fall.

The words in the pages of my *Orthodox Dogmatic Theology* book were no longer just words, but spiritual realities I was now experiencing in my mind, heart and soul. I learned that it was the transgression of Adam and Eve (Original Sin), which had permanently altered them and all their descendents, and the physical earth as well. Original Sin had altered me too; however, since my reentry into the Church, I had frequently experienced the sense of being free from the captivity of the fallen world.

Chapter 7

Amazing Grace

By now we were in the middle of Advent, which in the Orthodoxy begins on November 15ᵗʰ and ends on Christmas Day. "What is the purpose of Advent?" I asked my husband.

"Advent is the time set aside by the Church to prepare one's self for the birth of Christ. Our preparation gives us the possibility to prepare our soul, our metaphorical manger, to receive the Christ child. We abstain from certain foods and passions, to a lesser degree than during Lent, for forty days. We're striving to emulate Mary, who because she was so pure in body and spirit, became the dwelling place of God."

"How was that possible?" I asked. "I've known about Mary from my childhood, but I've always wondered how Mary remained a virgin, yet was married. Jesus had brothers and sisters – how could that be? I had all my issues getting to know and love Jesus, too. Could I truly be able prepare myself in such as way as to welcome Him into my soul? Could I finally find a way to open my heart to Christ?"

"Follow me," said Greg with a grin. We went to our bookshelves and he handed me yet another book to read, *The Life of Mary, The Theotokos* (Theotokos is Greek for "Mother of God").[17] "This book contains the oral traditions of the Orthodox Church about the life of Mary, and the sacred mysteries surrounding Christ's life, passed down from the early centuries of Christianity. It also includes beautiful hymnography and passages from the Holy Scriptures. "Reading this book should keep you busy for the entire fast and give me a chance to have a little peace and quiet!" Greg winked at me and left me to my new adventure.

Reading *The Life of Mary* was no small undertaking for me for it was hundreds of pages long. I hungrily devoured the preface and initial chapters of the book. I had read countless New Age and Gnostic renditions about the life of Mary, Christ and his followers in the past, but those who knew Christ and his mother had not written *those* books. The traditions contained in *The Life of Mary* had been passed down orally at first, and then were eventually put into writing by some of the greatest saints of the Church.

As I immersed myself in the Orthodox tradition about Mary's life, I found myself transported back to the person I was as an innocent child. If I had read these accounts prior to my conversion, I don't think my heart would have been as moved. As it was, I felt as if I were sitting on God's lap and He was reading to me. The sheer beauty of the poetic hymnography, combined with the amazing descriptions of miracles in the book, spoke to my soul, since I was now ready to absorb the spiritual significance of Mary's life.

My attraction to and love for Mary had continued through all my wanderings, even after I had stopped aspiring to a monastic vocation. Yet the stories in this book were all new and amazing to me. I learned about the miracles that had touched her parents prior to her birth, the depth and breath of Mary's purity, her encounters with angels, the overshadowing of the Holy Spirit for Christ's conception and the fulfillment of numerous Old Testament prophecies accomplished through Mary. No wonder Greg had winked at me when he handed me the book! It was all astounding.

"Could Mary's life truly be so pure and miraculous?" I wondered as I read. One year ago, my old skeptical and jaded self would have responded along these lines, "This biography is just too unbelievable. What I'm reading cannot be true. You have *got* to be kidding. How could anyone's life be this otherworldly, pure and blessed?" Yet, thanks to God, my desire to experience an intimate relationship with Christ and the sacred mysteries that had surrounded Mary's life overruled any inclination I might have had to judge what I was reading. Making false judgments had cost me dearly. Filled with God's love and spiritual warmth, I was convinced that these traditions of the Church were true.

Within the miracles and blessings that preceded Mary's life, I found an answer to a question that had long troubled me. Mary's birth, while miraculous for her parents (because they were in their 60s when they conceived Mary), was not an immaculate birth. This was a real revelation for me; since my early Catholic years, I had been taught that Mary was born immaculate, without sin, as Christ was born.

I asked my husband, "Was Mary born as any other human being?" Greg handed me yet another book, *The Orthodox Veneration of Mary, The Birthgiver of God*[18], written by St. John of Shanghai and San Francisco, which discussed the dogmatic differences between the Eastern and Western Churches regarding Mary. Since St. John was the same saint whose tomb Greg had visited the night before his longstanding wart disappeared, I read his writings carefully. St. John confirmed the validity of Mary's normal birth and discoursed about the spiritual significance of her immaculately lived life.

Mary lived a life in which she was always striving to acquire perfect love of God. She struggled with sin just as we all do, but her ardent love of God, her humble and repentant heart and her applied spiritual discipline, drew the grace of God to her. God's grace perfected Mary and she became a holy dwelling place in which God was conceived. As one of our Orthodox hymns expressed it: "He made your body into a throne and your womb became more spacious than the heavens".[19] Angels marveled at Mary's purity; she is considered by the Church to be higher than the angels!

Therefore, if it was possible for Mary, through her intense love of God, spiritual discipline and striving for virtue, to attain these heights, then sanctification was also possible for me! If Mary could do it – so could I! Granted, achieving even a minor level of sanctification would be a miracle for as wayward a child as myself, but with the amazing grace of God, my heart's desire from childhood was possible. In fact, the less perfect and the more humble, the better. Mary's own words resounded in my ears, "For he hath regarded the low estate of his handmaiden: for, behold, from henceforth all generations shall call me blessed." (Luke 1:48)

Knowing Mary was born as we all are, I could finally see myself in Mary and understand her role in God's Plan. Mary is the new Eve. She did what Eve could not do. Mary freely chose to love God with all her mind, heart and spirit despite, and through, any earthly struggles and temptations she experienced. She did not take her relationship with God for granted. Mary endured countless trials throughout her life, yet through all of them she remained faithful to God.

It was through Mary, a woman, that my personal redemption and the redemption of the world became possible! It was through her that the human race came to know God in the flesh. The highest honor and blessing that God could bestow upon any man was given to a woman. Mary became the source of salvation for all.

God had forgiven me, a fallen woman, and would continue to forgive me. I could now freely choose to follow Mary's example and the examples of countless other women saints in the Church. I did not have to be perfect for Christ to be born in the lowly manger of my soul. I certainly had my work cut out for me, but what a Christmas gift!

Chapter 8

Great Lent

As the first spring after my baptism approached, I felt I had adjusted to life as an Orthodox Christian. Still, the tension between my work and my new faith continued to challenge me. I was so close to completing my second book, *Channeling, a Bridge to Transcendence, Book II, Manifestation of Being*, that I felt compelled to finish. My editor, who was a friend, kept encouraging me to complete it, since we had been working on it for three years. He could sense that I was on the verge of another major life change that might very well keep me from wrapping up the project.

My second book was an amalgamation of many years of esoteric and metaphysical studies. In it, I transparently observed that I was *still* spiritually searching for something as I wrote the book, but what? Much of what I had studied and experienced about the life of the soul seemed to parallel Orthodox teachings, but I still hadn't resolved my confusions or questions about esoteric teachings and ascended masters in relation to Christ and the Church.

I also had questions about the validity of past life regressions. On faith, I had accepted the teaching that each person just has one lifetime, but I had not fully resolved my questions about past lives and reincarnation. If we live only one earthly life, what had I been doing, and where had I gone with my clients in our sessions when I led them through past life regressions? What about reincarnation? Twenty years of beliefs, history and relationships related to my former life did not simply disappear overnight after my baptism.

Claire and I were also struggling to find a new way to connect with each other. I knew that she, and the other staff members with whom I had worked, tried to understand my conversion, but we were all uncomfortable with my change and our spiritual paths felt somewhat disparate. I now felt a greater call to pursue my spiritual life in the Orthodox Church. I prayed that somehow through all the changes, we would remain friends.

It was with a heavy heart amidst these challenges that I began to prepare for Lent. Greg and my church friends explained that each year Great Lent, as it is called in the Orthodox Church, is a unique, remarkable spiritual journey within the cycle of the Church year. It's a time to reflect deeply upon what separates us from our Creator and others, and to seek the healing of God's grace for our fallen state. The ultimate purpose of our spiritual struggles during Great Lent and Holy Week is to prepare us for Pascha (Easter), the Resurrection of Christ. While I dreaded Lent, I was truly looking forward to having a new experience of the Resurrection.

The Orthodox Church provides a month of spiritual preparation before entering into Great Lent. The four Sundays preceding the first Monday of Lent set the tone for the penitential season. For the Eastern Church, Lent commences not on Ash Wednesday but on Clean Monday.

As the first day of Great Lent approached, I began to ask myself: could I humble myself anew, and see in the story of the prodigal son my own story? Was I truly aware of the consequences, short and long term, of pursuing my fallen will versus choosing God's will? How difficult would Lent be for me? This last question in particular led right to my biggest question, "Is my professional work, even with the changes I have made, truly bringing me closer to God and divine truth? Is this the work that God wants me to continue doing?"

In Orthodoxy, this fasting period is called 'Great Lent' and not simply 'Lent', for several reasons. It's the fast that is most strict and arduous in a church that loves fast days. [20] (Normally, Orthodox Christians fast every Wednesday and Friday as well.) As a child, I had resented Catholic fast days and grew to especially dislike fish on Fridays. Even though I had been a vegetarian for many years, it was little comfort to me as the first day of Great Lent approached. The Church taught that fasting from our negative passions was even more important than fasting from certain foods. According to the teachings of the Church, fasting was an opportunity to turn to God and choose to abstain from sinful behavior and thoughts, such as resentments and anger. Additionally, we were encouraged to give more financially to others who were less fortunate. "What you do not spend on food, give to the poor" wrote one sage. My church friends also advised me to delay making any major decisions until after Pascha (Easter). "Get your taxes done early. You don't want to deal with anything too distracting during Lent."

During my years of participating in seminars, I coined the term, "pre-seminar syndrome". Invariably, some struggle or personality weakness would surface a few weeks or days prior to the beginning of a workshop, to the point where I often became ill. As I prepared for six weeks of Lenten discipline, followed by Holy Week, I suffered a sort of "pre-Lent syndrome."

God would have to help me, but would I let Him? Could I find what my spirit was seeking in the desert of my fallen soul? Would I pass the Lenten test? Fortunately, my church friends humorously assured me that I would fail frequently and miserably. "This is not about being perfect because of your own efforts, Veronica. This is about being perfected in God." Thus, I entered into Great Lent with the theme of 'letting go of perfectionism' ringing in my ears.

Chapter 9

"Have mercy on me, oh God, have mercy on me."

The first week of Lent, Purification Week, is considered equal to Holy Week in terms of spiritual struggle and discipline. Purification Week sets the stage for one's learning and journey throughout Lent. Church services each day and evening are filled with remarkable hymnography, Old Testament readings and prayers structured to dismantle and reveal our hidden states of denial and separation. God quickly allowed me to see just how useless I was without Him. By the end of Great Lent's first day, Clean Monday, I was faint and fainthearted, voraciously hungry and despondent. All my years of being a vegetarian proved to be of no assistance. I craved everything I could not have and wanted to sleep the day away.

My state of stupor deepened as the week progressed despite my best efforts. Each night, we gathered in church for a service entitled the 'Great Canon', written by St. Andrew of Crete, which is divided into four parts spread out over the first four evenings of Lent. The hymnography of the Great Canon recounts different Biblical stories about Old and New Testament individuals, and how their stories teach us about our fallen nature. We sang "Have mercy on me, oh God, have mercy on me" repeatedly; this prolonged prayer literally brought me to my knees at times, for we frequently made prostrations as well during the service.

I had endured a 24-hour Tibetan fast with no food or water and also had performed hundreds of prostrations when studying Tibetan Buddhism. Yet my Buddhist experience paled next to the frustration, fatigue, hunger and dismay that I battled during the first few days of Great Lent. While my external prayers followed the week's theme, my internal prayers begged God for release as soon as possible and sounded more like this: "Dear God, can you help me get through these prayers, this service and this day so I can go to bed?" By Thursday night, I was reduced to a pitiful heap. Instead of enjoying a profound spiritual experience, I engaged in a prolonged, internal temper tantrum, with God as my object. "What do You want from me? I've been suffering for days. Do You even care? Why is this so hard?" Exhausted, I finally just gave up, sat down in church, tissue box in my lap, and sobbed and sobbed. Some of the congregation members were apparently worried that they had done something to offend me, although they also knew me well enough by then to know that I had an Italian flare for the dramatic!

When I had finally cried myself out, I began to listen to the prayers the other worshippers continued to chant. Now that I was still and quiet, the prayer "Have mercy on me, oh God, have mercy on me" began to echo in my soul. My heart started to open to the idea of asking God for mercy. What else could I do? My methods for seeking peace in the first week of the fast had been utterly ineffective.

"Have mercy on me, oh God, have mercy on me." "Be still and know that I am God." (Ps. 46:10) My soul waited, humbled. "Have mercy on me, oh God, have mercy on me." Then, imperceptibly, softly, I perceived I was no longer alone. "Could that be you, Lord, entering the door of my heart? Could I finally be still enough to feel Your Presence? "Have mercy on me, oh God, have mercy on me." Instead of tears of anger, tears of quiet joy streamed down my cheeks. "Have mercy on me, oh God, have mercy on me." I sat quietly and felt His Presence in my heart while the prayer, "Have mercy on me, oh God, have mercy on me," further permeated my being.

Once again, I saw that without God's tender mercies, I was nothing but my cravings, desires and angry, egotistical self. I didn't truly understand what God had in mind for me through this prolonged season of fasting and prayer, but now He had my attention. I had hope, now, that God would show me the way if I humbly allowed Him into my heart and soul, and I left the service that night at peace with Him. I had stumbled and crawled my way through the first Lenten challenges

Chapter 10

Sickness of Soul

After the first week of Great Lent, I began to perceive that a veil covered the eyes of my soul. My initial struggles with the sobriety of fasting and prayer during Purification Week had started to pierce this state of illusion and compromised spiritual vision, but still I wondered, what was this illusion?

In that week of services, we'd read from Genesis, "And God formed man of dust of the earth, and breathed upon his face the breath of life, and the man became a living soul." (Gen: 2:7) I pondered these words, especially the last phrase…became a living soul." I had never quite forgotten Who had given my soul to me, even during my years of wandering and running from God, even as I had tried to forget that the source of my life was, and is, God. The study of the soul had fascinated me since my early 20s; I spent years reading every non-Christian, metaphysical book or article that I could find which touched on this subject. As a New Age spiritual teacher, I had prided myself on the fact that I had so much knowledge about the soul.

Now I was stumped. "Why do Orthodox Christians associate acts of sin with the soul, rather than with the ego? Why do the prayers and hymnography keep referring to the soul as being in danger or asleep?" We sang, "My soul, my soul, my soul, why art thou sleeping? The end is approaching and soon thou shalt be troubled. Awake therefore, that

Christ our God may save thee. Who is everywhere present and fillest all things."[21]

Greg listened, ever patient, to my questions. "How can my soul be sick, if it is immortal and given to me by God?"

"That's an important question," answered Greg. "I think it's time for you to read another book. Then let's have this conversation." Greg placed *A Spiritual Life*, by St. Theophan, in my hand.

When reading Orthodox materials, I typically ended up with more questions than answers. In *A Spiritual Life*, St. Theophan, a highly respected and quoted 19th century Russian Christian, wrote that the interests of our soul are often *not* seeking our highest good. "But how could that be true?" I asked myself. Moved by desires, thoughts and senses, the soul, according to St. Theophan, is in constant motion and cannot stay still.[22] This also surprised me, for I thought it was my mind that had difficulty being at peace, not my soul. Wasn't that what most meditative and New Age teachers claimed? I thought it was my ego that preyed on my mind, but according to St. Theophan, it was the soul that was strictly concerned with temporal life and with keeping us comfortable and protected.

St. Theophan went on to explain that the soul, when in its lower expression, is submerged in earthly concerns and devoted to the gratification of its temporal needs, which, in turn, causes it to be greatly inclined towards sin. I took some time to digest this; as I prayed and pondered St. Theophan's teaching, I felt as if the foundation upon which I had built twenty years of spiritual awareness was being gutted.

It occurred to me that my belief that my ego was the primary troublemaker had allowed me to address behavior problems, but this belief had also apparently prevented me from seeing a much deeper spiritual reality. I had thought that my soul was concerned only with my higher good. Not so, according to the Church! My ego and soul apparently had been sharing the same bed for years! I had revered my soul as my personal God. Why would I need God, if my soul thinks it is perfect? The Freudian definition of the ego is flawed, I learned, for it bypasses the relationship of the soul to our ego; in truth, our soul is as much a part of our lower nature as the ego.

No wonder my husband and others were so worried about me before I converted. I was in danger of losing my soul, which was all wrapped up in my fleshly ego! No wonder that the hymns and prayers we chant consistently strive to remind us of our fallen condition – to wake us up! "My soul, my soul, my soul, why art thou sleeping? The end is approaching and soon thou shalt be troubled. Awake therefore, that Christ our God may save thee." I understood now!

St. Theophan went on to describe three aspects of the soul, which have both a fallen expression and a spiritual, heavenly expression.[23] "Ouch! That hurt!" I said, upon reading his descriptions of the lower aspects of the soul. During my Hindu experiences, I had learned how to focus my awareness on my third eye while breathing, doing yoga or using mantras or visualizations to quiet my mind and relax my body. I usually entered into a blissful, expansive space, which I had thought was the serenity of my soul. However, after reading what St. Theophan and other saints of the Church had to say about the questionable and deceptive nature of these states of bliss, I began to wonder. "What was my soul actually doing? Where was my soul actually going?"

St. Theophan emphasized that there was a distinction between feeling good (a lower expression of the soul) and truly experiencing the Holy Spirit. Channeling, for me, had been based on feelings that were sensual, even sexual at times. As a budding channel, I was encouraged to feel not only with my sixth sense, my third eye, but also with my whole body, while reaching for the so-called higher planes and realities. Many New Age practices are also based on trusting your inner feelings and intuitions, without regard for where the trust is actually being placed. I had felt such a sense of elation and power during my channeling sessions, which I equated to having achieved some measure of enlightenment.

As I pondered this further, I recalled how much I had craved more of these experiences, similar to when one craves chocolate or sex. My students and I hungered for the next breakthrough, which to us meant that we were transforming, evolving and achieving our spiritual goals. We were passionate about our desires, but was our passion misdirected and misplaced? Did we truly experience transformation?" According to St. Theophan and the teachings of the Church, we had missed the mark.

Not only had I desired these special states of being, I realized that I also had craved the acknowledgement I received from teaching others how to achieve the same experiences. "Could these so-called transformational states of bliss and awareness in actuality have seduced my soul into a state self-delusion? What about the information I had gained while in these sensual states and movements? What about the ascended masters taking me into these states? "Have mercy on me, oh God! Have mercy on me." As the realization of what I had done overwhelmed me, I was reduced to yet another groaning lump on the floor.

According to the saints of the Church, if man had not fallen, our soul's yearnings would naturally have brought us closer to God, for they would have been pure. In a fallen world, however, in which a state of separation from God is the norm, we frequently miss the mark. We enter into the fallen world at birth, our soul can become imprisoned in its lower state and our spirit slowly dies, as the innocence of our spirit and our memory of connection with our true home fades. I had searched for relief from my sickness of soul through whatever spiritual techniques and studies came my way, but they had produced more sickness of the same. No wonder I had still thirsted in my spirit!

Chapter 11

My Soul Wakes Up!

As I prayed and moved on in my studies throughout the remainder of Lent, I had to admit some hard truths about my past actions and the state of my soul. My abstinence and prayers during Lent illumined how much I loved self-gratification. Throughout my twenty plus years of seeking, I had immersed myself in spiritual look-a-likes, which I thought would fulfill my spiritual desires. I had learned a measure of discipline and mindfulness[37] through my Eastern and metaphysical studies, but I had not learned or practiced true dispassion.[24] The teachings, techniques and mantras I had learned had helped me enter into meditative states but according to St. Theophan, I was not contemplating the Divine in these states, but was unknowingly fostering a deepening state of self-deception.

I had the desire to be one with God, but only occasionally was my soul truly *with* God. True dispassion is a lifelong journey that is not possible without an active, healthy relationship with God. Since I was primarily feeding the lower aspects of my soul, it was always craving something new and different. Since I had been committed to doing things my way, I couldn't dwell in God. I hated to admit that I had not truly wanted a real relationship with God until my conversion. I had lacked the voluntary inclination to bend my will towards obeying God's will, unless I was ill. Talk about being stubborn! It took the horror of seeing a devil to begin to alert me to the dangerous condition of my soul.

After soberly acknowledging my true spiritual state, I felt a sense of relief and freedom. The truth shall set you free! My newly born freedom gave me room to breathe and the courage to move on to the next battle that awaited me. Throughout my Lenten journey, while grappling with my understandings about the soul and its passions, I somehow completed writing my second book, with the help of my editor and friend.

Striving to complete my second book had been a struggle for midway through its completion, I began my conversion. I felt as though I had been living in two worlds - one when I was in church and prayer, another when I was writing or teaching. Keeping my promise to my friend, I finished the book on the last Friday of Lent.

"What am I going to do with this book now that it's done?" I asked God in prayer. "Where am I heading with my professional life? What do You want me to do? Have mercy on me, oh God! Have mercy on me! This is too overwhelming for me to figure out. Dear Lord, will You show me the way? I don't know what to do with my work. I'm scared. Please help me."

That evening and the next morning, I went to special services which commemorated Christ's miraculous raising of Lazarus back to life after he had been dead for four days. Reflecting upon the healing of Lazarus, I had to ask God, "How could healing occur for my students and me, since we were apparently using the lower senses of our soul in our sessions and classes?"

I pondered the deep bond of love and intimacy my students and I had formed and shared throughout our spiritual strivings together. Love comes from God. Therefore, I could see that we were with God in the spirit of our love. I had become close friends with many of my students and clients. We cared for each other. We expressed deep concern for each other and helped each other bear our struggles. At the beginning of our sessions or classes, we would discuss the problems we hoped to remedy while setting healing and transformational goals for the outcome of our work.

I recalled that the sessions that produced an outcome of healing occurred when we had expressed authentic sorrow and regret for our unhealthy thoughts, beliefs and actions. Based on all that I had now studied in Orthodox Christianity, I began to hopefully conclude that at least the loving and repentant nature of our work together had been spiritually sound. In our own way, we had acknowledged our state of separation and error. We had regretted the consequences of our actions resulting from our fallen state and had expressed our sincere desire to change while supporting one another. Again, I asked God the same question, "How could healing occur for my students and me, since we were apparently using the lower senses of our soul in our sessions and classes?"

I suddenly realized that it was not through our guides, personal will, spiritual prowess or degree of enlightenment that healing had occurred. Shockingly, I now understood that any healing that occurred from our work together was solely the result of God's compassion and love for us. Sadly, I had to admit that we had given the credit for our healing to our guides, our gurus, the universe or ourselves, but never to the Author of all good, God Himself. In tears, ashamed and humbled, I cried out, "How could I have forgotten the Source of my life for so long? How could I have not seen the true Light? Forgive me. Have mercy on me, oh God, have mercy on me." God had unselfishly loved me, despite my spiritual arrogance and almost total lack of love for or awareness of Him.

I had thanked God so seldomly during my wandering years, unless it was a casual, "Thank God!" A sincere, heartfelt expression of gratitude towards God had been a consistent challenge for me to utter. "How could I have been so blind? How could I not have seen that God was with me and had cared for me, even when I rarely had any thought of Him?"

"Have mercy on me, oh God, have mercy on me." My soul was now beginning to truly wake up.

Chapter 12

"Why are we here again?"

During Lent, the Church's Scripture readings are from the Old Testament, especially those related to The Fall and the events that foreshadowed the coming of the Messiah. As I attended the significant, life altering services each day and evening during Holy Week, my heart finally began to open to the enormity of Christ's mission on earth. Clearly, the events that occurred during Christ's life, especially the last week of his life, were prophesized in numerous passages of the Old Testament by significant spiritual figures such as Isaiah, Jeremiah, King David and many others.

These prophecies included:

- Jesus' miraculous healings of the blind, deaf and infirm
- His raising of Lazarus and others from the dead
- Christ's entry into Jerusalem on the colt of an ass
- The inability of the Jewish elders to let Christ into their hearts and their jealousies
- Judas's betrayal of Christ for thirty pieces of silver
- The scattering of Christ's apostles
- The lots cast for Christ's robe
- The vinegar and gall Christ was given to drink on the cross

During Holy Week, the Old Testament is fulfilled. A new covenant is formed with God through Christ, and a New Testament emerges in Christ. The redemption from our fall required an effort that even the most righteous individuals before Christ were unable to achieve. "Blessed are the pure in heart for they shall see God." (Matt. 5:8) I began to understand that the effects of our fall from grace required an act of love that we, as human beings, were incapable of achieving until Christ.

Our Lenten readings from the Old Testament witness to humanity's continual losing battle with our passions (our negative passions, which the Holy Fathers simply call "passions"). I finally accepted the fact that my soul had been blind to its own precarious position. "I get it God. This is a journey we are making together. I am finally here! I understand that my ongoing battle with passions and my soul's weaknesses are real. I understand that I cannot escape this battle. Thanks to You, my arsenal of spiritual weapons, which I desperately sought when I returned from Auschwitz, is growing. I can even hold a reasonably calm dialogue with You now. So, can You please explain to me why I am still resisting The Cross?"

A sense of dread descended upon me. Holy Week had finally brought me to Good Friday. I could not stand to be with myself. "Polly, what is your problem?" I said to myself. "Why are you so uncomfortable with Good Friday? What is bothering you?" My inner self responded, "Can I just run away now?" I was as uncomfortable in this moment as I was when I ran out of my first Orthodox service, tears streaming down my face.

"I have been trying to get your attention all week," continued my inner dialogue. "Do you remember how you dreaded Good Friday when you were young?"

Sort of," I responded.

"Then why are we here again? Do you remember how you wept throughout the entire service every year? How you felt completely drained and empty when the Stations of the Cross were finally over?" The pain of my Good Friday memories now descended upon me. "Yes, I'm starting to remember." My inner child had my full attention now. "Good. Remember how the nuns and priests told you over and over again that it was because of you and your sins that Christ died? We were supposed to have been saved by His death, but all we felt was confused, guilty and sad."

"Good point," I responded.

The traumatic memories were returning. When Easter arrived, two days after Holy Friday, I had never been able to truly celebrate. We could finally eat meat, dress up, hunt for Easter eggs and watch a special movie on television such as "Easter Parade". "Remember how you were supposed to feel joyful about Christ's resurrection? But you weren't joyful, you were filled with sorrow, pain and bitterness."

I was crying as the sadness of those days returned. I didn't want to think about it but I had no choice. "What don't you want to see, Polly? What are you running from this time?"

Then, oh so slowly, I heard my inner self say, "Christ died a horrible death. His death was somehow my fault. And... I do not... I do not... believe that anything happened after Christ died. Otherwise, I would have changed, right? The world would have been different. Someone around me would have said something besides "Happy Easter", right? There, I have said it! Do you understand?"

When both my inner child and grown up self had calmed down, I began to pray for guidance for how to address this issue. As we rested during the prayers, words started to form inside my heart and I whispered to my inner child, "I know this sounds crazy to you, but we are here to experience something altogether different. I know this is hard for you, but you need to trust me. God will help both of us understand why He died on the cross, why His death was not in vain. God will help us heal." Then there was silence.

I continued to pray until my inner child whispered back, "Okay. Will you promise me that this time will be different?"

I prayed and took a few deep breaths. "Yes, I trust that this Good Friday will be different, because I trust God and the Church now. I'm different inside now. You've seen the changes in me over the last few months. God has answered all my silent prayers. He knows my heart and what we need to heal. This is why I became Orthodox. I want to truly know why Christ died on The Cross. I want to grasp what is not logically understandable about His Death. I want to believe in The Resurrection." [25]

My inner child had finally calmed down. I could finally relax. Greg had just arrived home, "It's time to go. You're not even dressed yet! Well, neither am I! Oh, you've been crying again." Greg gave me a hug.

"It's okay, honey," I replied. "I'll give you all the details in the car. I'm truly ready to go to our Good Friday service. Let's get dressed!" As we drove into San Francisco, I told Greg my story. We pulled up to the curb and I gave him a big smile and a kiss. As he drove off to park the car, I raced down the stairs to our little chapel for the Good Friday service, a glimmer of hope now rising in my heart.

Chapter 13

The Cross

The beauty of our little chapel took my breath away. It was still shrouded in black, for we were mourning the death of our Lord. My journey that began one month before Lent had brought me to the cross. On Holy Friday, the Church asks worshippers to adhere to the strictest fast possible, according to one's strength. Great Lent had toughened me up and I was more prepared for this holy day than I would have been otherwise.

Those who are not Orthodox wonder why we have such a desire to follow the ancient traditions and rituals of the early Church. This was my query as well until my conversion. The early saints of the Church formed our traditions based on the doctrines and teachings of Christ, many of which were not written in books, but passed down orally from the Apostles to their disciples, then to their disciples and onward through the ages.

With the Holy Spirit guiding them, the Holy Fathers and Mothers of the Church understood the need for discipline and tradition, especially as the Roman Empire legalized Christianity. Many fled to the deserts of Sinai and to the forests and mountain caves to escape faddish Christianity. In solitude, these saintly souls learned and practiced sacred dispassion and thus acquired the grace of the Holy Spirit. Many lost their lives defending the Truth and Traditions of Ancient Christianity, as different heresies manifested to challenge the early Church. These heresies tested the Church and her saints and Great Ecumenical Councils were formed, in which the core of our sacred theology and traditions were laid forth.

We, as modern Orthodox Christians, have inherited the fruits of their labors. The beauty of Orthodox icons and churches, the depth of the services, the structured chanting and hymnography, as well as a tested and faithful tradition of asceticism continuing to the present day, were created by the saints of the Church, through divine revelation, for the eyes of our souls (*nous*)[26] I was grateful for all their efforts now, as I stood before the cross on Holy Friday. How many souls had contributed to my ability to enter into the Sacred Mysteries of the Church? How many?

As I silently venerated[27] the cross, so lovingly adorned with flowers, I thought of my past. Flowers had been part of my life from the moment my mother placed me, her newborn child, in a gardenia box. What a gift God had given me, through my parents, to be surrounded by flowers! Flowers bring joy, hope and courage to those who are sick and suffering. They are a beautiful reminder that God is present, even in the darkest moments of our lives.

As the service began, my mind drifted back to Auschwitz, where I had witnessed one of the ultimate expressions of evil passion. Now I stood, witnessing with Christians throughout the world, remembering how every imaginable sin of the human race was brought to bear upon Christ. Not a word of anger, not an action of malice or thought of resentment, did Christ commit in return. Christ's voluntary Passion was, and is, the quintessential expression of dispassion.

As the Holy Friday chants and Scriptures continued, I began to feel as if time had stopped. Though Christ had endured his sufferings and death 2,000 years prior, I felt as though I were with Him again as he, an innocent man, of his own free will, was mocked, humiliated, tortured and crucified. There were countless times when Christ could have opted out of his journey to the cross. He knew what was coming and spoke openly about his approaching death with his disciples on many occasions.[28]

Through our prayers and hymns, I was with Him, standing below the cross. I was no longer the young girl in unbearable pain, however, but a soul alive in Christ through my conversion. The realization dawned on me that I had come to love what I had dreaded, even hated.

Then I heard the voice of our pastor. "Jesus, when he had cried again with a loud voice, yielded up the ghost. And behold, the veil of the temple was rent in twain from the top to the bottom; and the earth did quake, and the rocks rent; and the graves were opened; and many bodies of the saints which slept arose, and came out of the graves after his Crucifixion, and went into the holy city, and appeared unto many. Now when the centurion, and they that were with him, watching Jesus, saw the earthquake, and those things that were done, they feared greatly, saying, 'Truly this was the Son of God'." (Math 27:50-54) I hadn't remembered ever reading about the eyewitness reports from the Gospels of what had occurred after Christ had died. People had witnessed the release of the souls of the righteous! The centurion who had stabbed Christ with a spear had testified to what he had seen.[29]

Reverently, our pastor carried an exquisite embroidered icon of Our Lord lying in the tomb to the center of the church and placed it below the cross. Our choir continued to sing a beautiful hymn describing the gentle care with which Joseph of Arimathaea took Christ's body down from the cross, anointed it and placed it in a new tomb. We prayed in silence. Our priest then spoke to our sorrow and the significance of this moment.

"Yes, we are lamenting Christ's voluntary death, and will continue to do so into the wee hours of the evening[30], but this is not the end. As God-Man, Christ was free from sin, but tempted by it. He understood our struggles. Christ condescended as God to become one with us, so that perhaps by our free will and by learning to live a dispassionate life, we could one day become one with Him again in Paradise. He gave up his life for all of us. He reconciled the fall of man from grace through his sinless, grace-filled life and passionless death. Christ's death was necessary to free each of us from the consequences of sin and the death of the soul through the passions.

Father continued, "We are here to humbly venerate and acknowledge Christ's voluntary dispassionate suffering and love for mankind. Through Christ's voluntary death, we are freed from the death of sin! 'His death has become our life!'[31] As Christ's human body died, Christ as God descended into hell and freed all the souls of the righteous that had been held captive since the falling asleep of Adam and Eve. Paradise was and is reclaimed! The redemptive miracle of Christ's voluntary death set fallen mankind free from the death of sin then and now! Let us come forth now and lovingly venerate our long suffering Lord."

I then joined the congregants as we prostrated and venerated the icon of Christ lying in the tomb. Yes, it was Good Friday! Yes, I was still in tears, for who would wish such a death for a true friend or any human being? But my sorrow was now mixed with profound gratitude, expectation and joy. My pastor's words rang in my ears, "The redemptive miracle of Christ's voluntary death set fallen mankind free from the death of sin then and now!"

When I tuned into my inner child, I could see that she was thrilled! By coming to peace with sin and Christ's triumph over it, I finally felt released from guilt. When I finally collapsed into my bed late that night, I also realized I had had my first true experience of "the peace that passes all understanding". (Phil 4:7) In my heart, I finally understood what I had missed my entire adult life. I believed!

Chapter 14

Pascha

It was now Holy Saturday morning. As I helped others put the finishing touches on the meal we would be sharing after our service, one friend asked, "Isn't it wonderful that your mother is going to be baptized and received into the Orthodox Church today, Veronica?"

"Yes, after all the changes my mom witnessed in me, she wants to convert, too. My mom wasn't sure if she had ever been baptized as a child." Indeed, we had searched for any record of a Protestant baptism but there was none to be found.

"How old is your mom?" my friend asked.

"She is the ripe age of seventy-three!" I responded, chuckling.

"You've got to be kidding! Both your mom and dad look so young."

"Yes! My dad is almost ninety!" I marveled. The fact that both my mom and dad started coming to our church after my baptism was something I never expected. They fell in love with our little church and community.

"What a blessing for all of us" my friend replied. This was so true, as my parents had become an integral part of our parish.

Words cannot describe my joy as I watched my mom being dipped in the baptismal waters, which was in and of itself a big deal, for my mom truly disliked putting her head under water. Once the baptism was completed and my mom had rejoined us after drying off and putting on her baptismal gown, our congregation settled down for a series of Old Testament readings. Parishioners read selections from Genesis and other Old Testament books witnessing to the history of mankind from creation and The Fall, to Noah and the Ark, through the exodus of the Jewish people from Egypt, to the prophecies of Isaiah, Jeremiah, and Daniel, and onward – fifteen passages all together.

I especially loved the story of Israel's miraculous escape from the Egyptians during the first Passover. The night before the Jews fled Egypt, they were instructed by God, through Moses, to eat lamb and smear the blood of the lamb on their doors. This is how the angel of death would know to pass over their homes, sparing them from the final plague God was to give to Egypt – the death of each Egyptian first-born son because Pharaoh refused to let the Jewish people go.

Moses led his people to the Red Sea – a seeming dead end. At the command of God, Moses parted the waters and led God's chosen people cross the sea onto dry land until they were safe. Meanwhile, the waters of the sea closed in behind them and destroyed Pharaoh and his whole army. (Exodus 13:20-15:19) This story prefigures our salvation in spirit, from our captivity by sin to our liberation from slavery to the fallen world. Christ is our new Passover, "The Lamb of God who takes away the sins of the world."[32]

These readings gave me a window into the mystery of God's plan and providence for humanity. Events that happened to the chosen people in the Old Testament demonstrate the relationship between God's Old and New Covenants. "Where had I been all these years?" My heart, as was true for Pharaoh's heart, had been hardened. I, too, had "eyes that could not see and ears that could not hear."[33] I had judged the Old Testament as insignificant for thirty years. I was quite mistaken. The prophecies were, indeed, true and fulfilled in Christ.

Each reading built upon the next, until our Holy Saturday Service suddenly burst forth in triumphal joy and we sang, "And gloriously has He been glorified!" The black vestments and coverings that had been present throughout Lent were removed. Everything was now white, symbolizing Christ's triumph over death. Then our Liturgy service began; "Let all mortal flesh keep silent and in fear and trembling stand. Offering nothing earthly minded, for the King of kings and the Lord of lords, comes to be slain, to give Himself as food for the faithful…"[34] The Orthodox proclaim many times in the liturgy that Christ's body and blood become mystically present in the chalice, by the grace of the Holy Spirit, as the priest prepares what is called "The Lamb".[35] As a catechumen, I watched others receive Communion and sensed the presence of Christ in the Eucharist, for I saw that those who received were transformed.

Now my mom, lit candle in hand, with my dad faithfully at her side, received her Chrismation and first Holy Communion. There was not a dry eye in our little chapel. After a well-earned meal and celebration of my mom's baptismal day, we all retired to rest before our midnight Paschal service.

The Orthodox Easter service is called Pascha because it means Passover. Christ is our new Passover, for He, the voluntary sacrificial Lamb for our sins, has passed over from death to life. Just as Holy Communion is the crowning jewel of the sacraments, Pascha is the holy Feast of all Feasts, for it is the feast of the resurrection of Christ. Our Paschal Matins service begins at 11:00 p.m. and ends around 2:00 a.m.

The church was dimly lit as we entered that night and quiet in anticipation. The beautifully embroidered icon of Christ lying in the tomb still rested in the center of our chapel. The choir began singing hymns. At a certain point, from behind the iconostasis (the wall with icons of Christ and Mary and other icons depicting the holy feasts and many Saints of the Church), our priest emerged and retrieved the embroidered icon and returned it to the sanctuary, placing it on the altar.

He then reemerged with a lit candle from which we began to light each of the candles we were holding. All of the parishioners and clergy then participated in a processional three times around the outside of the church, all of us in song, with candles lit. The priest then knocked on the door of the Church three times and declared, "Christ is Risen!" We responded, "In truth He is Risen!" The priest opened the door to the temple and we entered into a brilliantly lit church singing, "Christ is risen from the dead, trampling down death by death and upon those in the tombs bestowing life!" We continued singing about the miraculous resurrection of Christ and our freedom from death and sin throughout the service, which ended with Holy Communion. "Now all is filled with light, Heaven and Earth and the lower regions. Let all creation celebrate the rising of Christ in whom we are established."

I tried to speak but I could barely verbalize anything other than, "Honey, Honey, wake up! Something is happening!" Then I fell to the floor, sobbing with an uncontainable joy. "I am filled and surrounded by Light! I am filled and surrounded by Light! I am so unworthy. Oh God, I am so unworthy! Christ is Risen! Christ is Risen!" [36]

Epilogue

Then what happened?

"Then what happened?" Good question! I have attempted to answer this question in a short chapter, but each time my husband would read what I had written, he would say, "You need to write a sequel!" I resisted this for a time, but then realized that he was right. Therefore, dear reader, please forgive me! This is not the end, but rather the beginning of my second book! May God bless you on your spiritual journey until we meet again! Christ is Risen! Indeed, He is Risen!

The End

Appendix I -

Setting the RecordStraight
My "Readers Digest" version of the "The Life of Mary"
until the conception of Christ.

(Based on oral and written traditions of the Eastern Orthodox Church)

Mary was the daughter of Joachim and Anna, a devout elderly Jewish couple who were childless. Both prayed continually that God would grant them a child, yet not until they were both well over sixty years old, did God miraculously answer their prayers. (Miraculous conceptions were frequently documented in the Old Testament in answer to the prayers of devout, elderly Jewish couples, such as Abraham and Sarah.) Each, independently, received a visitation from the angel Gabriel. He informed them that they would give birth to a little girl who would eventually become the mother of the Messiah.

As was the Jewish custom in those days, the first-born child, male or female, was given to God. Usually an animal sacrifice was offered instead of literally giving one's child to God. Anna, however, had promised Mary to God in her prayers and at the tender age of three, Mary was brought to the temple, to be of service to God. (*The Entry of the Theotokos* into the temple is a beautiful feast celebrated in the Church at the beginning of Advent.) Virgins holding lit candles lined the steps as Mary walked without her parents into the temple. Then Mary did something quite unusual. She walked directly into the *Holy of Holies*, the altar where customarily no women were allowed! Since several of the priests in the temple were aware of Gabriel's visitation to Mary's parents and his prophetic words regarding Mary, they did not obstruct her path. Then something even more astounding occurred. An angel appeared to Mary, fed her and instructed her to return to the *Holy of Holies* to receive instruction and spiritual food daily!

As was the custom, when young girls reached the age to marry, they left the temple to do just that. Jewish women had to be married. They also needed to bear children, for the Messiah could potentially come from one of their offspring. That is why Mary's elderly parents had continued to entreat God for a child. Because Mary's parents had been reposed for several years, she was a ward of the temple.

When Mary came of age, she refused to marry. Mary desired to remain a virgin, for she valued her relationship with God above all things of this world, even to the point of insisting that the Jewish elders and priests preserve her virginity. Mary's desire to remain a virgin posed a unique problem for the Jewish elders.

Their solution to Mary's request was to select an older man from their community to become her husband, a man who would honor her desire to remain a virgin. It was Joseph, a widower eighty years old, who was chosen to be her husband by a miraculous series of events.

Joseph had seven children from his first marriage, which is how it came to be that Jesus had brothers and sisters. I am not sure how Joseph's age was somehow altered in the West, but this is the tradition preserved in the Eastern Orthodox Church. Joseph was not the young man as portrayed today in many of the modern images of the Holy Family. He was over 100 years old when he reposed.

Soon after Mary was betrothed to Joseph, the angel Gabriel appeared to her again. He greeted Mary with this salutation, "Hail! Thou who art full of grace, the Lord is with thee, blessed art thou among women." He then proceeds to tell her that she has been chosen by God. "And behold thou shalt conceive in thy womb, and bring forth a son, and thou shalt call his name JESUS. He shall be great, and shall be called the Son of the Highest; and the Lord God shall give unto him the throne of his father David... Then Mary said unto the angel, 'How shall this be, seeing I am not with a man'? The angel answered and said unto her, 'The Holy Ghost shall come upon thee and the power of the Highest shall overshadow thee. . . . therefore, also that holy thing which shall be born of thee shall be called the Son of God. . .For with God nothing is impossible. And Mary said, 'Behold the handmaid of the Lord, be it done unto me according to thy word.' And the angel departed from her." (Luke 1:28-38)

Mary did become pregnant, but Joseph was not the paternal father of Christ. By the overshadowing of the Holy Spirit, Mary conceived without seed, without intimate relations with a man! This is one of the great mysteries of the church. Thus, Mary remained a virgin during the conception of Jesus. This was the fulfillment of a prophecy made by Isaiah, "Therefore the Lord Himself shall give you a sign, behold a virgin shall conceive, and bear a son, and shall call his name Immanuel." (Is 7:14)

This brief summary of the early life of Mary and the miraculous conception of Christ clarified the confusion I had experienced as a child and teenager relating to the Holy Family. The Western Catholic version of Mary's life did not make sense to me – given that Christ had brothers and sisters.

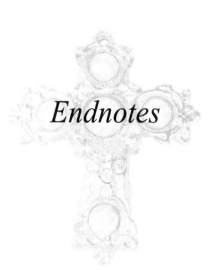

Endnotes

1. *A labyrinth is a circular puzzle, an intricate structure of interconnecting passages one walks on, in, or through.*

2. *Walking the Chartres labyrinth, seekers are guided by a group of prayerful questions related to one's relationship with and journey to God. Each turn presents an opportunity for one to ponder an aspect of one's relationship with God. Finding the center of the labyrinth with these guided steps helps the pilgrim ponder what it means to be with God. One's journey is not over when one reaches the center of the labyrinth; rather, reaching the center is only the first half of the journey. One's return or exit from the labyrinth is intended to bring what one has learned relative to God back into one's life—a life hopefully more devoted to God.*

3. ***What is the Eastern Orthodox Church?***
   The Eastern Orthodox Catholic Church is the Catholic Church established by Christ and his apostles during the first century of Christianity. Until 1054 AD, when the first schism in the Church occurred, there was only one Catholic Church. What caused this schism to happen? The divisions between the Eastern and Western Churches had been brewing for several centuries. Geographically, Rome was a considerable distance and

more isolated from the other established Christian centers in Jerusalem, Egypt, Constantinople and Antioch. This separation combined with foreign invasions, growing cultural differences, power struggles and significant doctrinal differences eventually forced a split.

The Eastern Orthodox Catholic Church remained true to all the original doctrines and practices of the early church, while the Western Catholic Church did not. With each split from the Western Catholic Church, more changes in the fundamental beliefs and doctrines occurred, until now we have a multitude of Christian faiths with an astounding number of different religious practices and beliefs, some of which are related to the early Church.

4. ***St. John of Shanghai and San Francisco***

   He was originally born in Russia, in 1896. As a young man, he went to law school and later felt the call to become a priest. He was consecrated a Bishop and sent to China after WWII. Blessed John founded an orphanage for abandoned infants and children whom he rescued on his daily journeys throughout the streets of Shanghai. He was fearless in the face of adversity when the communists took over China. He arranged safe passage for his entire flock to the Philippine island of Tubabao. Then Blessed John came to America, where he made arrangements for all his spiritual children to immigrate to America.

   Throughout his life, he healed countless people from life threatening illnesses. He rarely slept in his later years. Blessed John was humble and meek, going without shoes and eating once a day. He did not conform to people's ideas of a bishop and was consequently persecuted by those who were jealous of him. Blessed John's remains were kept in a beautiful chapel below the cathedral after his repose in 1966. Before his canonization, when his original casket was opened, his remains were found to be incorrupt. This means that they did not decay and this is one of the signs that a pious individual has achieved sainthood.

5. *Introduction to "The Path of Prayer" by St. Theophan, Preface*

6. *(Etymology: Middle English, from Anglo-French, from Latin humilis low, humble; from humus earth, not proud or haughty: not arrogant or assertive; reflecting, expressing, or offered in a spirit of deference or submission.).*

7. *"Once the remembrance of God has been established in the inner man, then Christ the Lord will dwell within you. The two things go together. A certain warm feeling toward the Lord will serve as a sign to convince you that this most wonderful thing has begun to operate inside of you." A Spiritual Life pg. 222-23*

8. *St. Mary of Egypt, St Nectarios Press*

9. ### *The Prodigal Son*

   [11] And he said, A certain man had two sons:

   [12] And the younger of them said to his father, Father, give me the portion of goods that falleth to me. And he divided unto them his living.

   [13] And not many days after the younger son gathered all together, and took his journey into a far country, and there wasted his substance with riotous living.

   [14] And when he had spent all, there arose a mighty famine in that land; and he began to be in want.

   [15] And he went and joined himself to a citizen of that country; and he sent him into his fields to feed swine.

   [16] And he would fain have filled his belly with the husks that the swine did eat: and no man gave unto him.

   [17] And when he came to himself, he said, How many hired servants of my father's have bread enough and to spare, and I perish with hunger!

   [18] I will arise and go to my father, and will say unto him, Father, I have sinned against heaven, and before thee,

   [19] And am no more worthy to be called thy son: make me as one of thy hired servants.

   [20] And he arose, and came to his father. But when he was yet a great way off, his father saw him, and had compassion, and ran, and fell on his neck, and kissed him.

   [21] And the son said unto him, Father, I have sinned against heaven, and in thy sight, and am no more worthy to be called thy son.

   [22] But the father said to his servants, Bring forth the best robe, and put it on him; and put a ring on his hand, and shoes on his feet:

   [23] And bring hither the fatted calf, and kill it; and let us eat, and be merry:

[24] *For this my son was dead, and is alive again; he was lost, and is found. And they began to be merry.*

[25] *Now his elder son was in the field: and as he came and drew nigh to the house, he heard music and dancing.*

[26] *And he called one of the servants, and asked what these things meant.*

[27] *And he said unto him, Thy brother is come; and thy father hath killed the fatted calf, because he hath received him safe and sound.*

[28] *And he was angry, and would not go in: therefore came his father out, and entreated him.*

[29] *And he answering said to his father, Lo, these many years do I serve thee, neither transgressed I at any time thy commandment: and yet thou never gavest me a kid, that I might make merry with my friends:*

[30] *But as soon as this thy son was come, which hath devoured thy living with harlots; thou hast killed for him the fatted calf.*

[31] *And he said unto him, Son, thou art ever with me, and all that I have is thine.*

[32] *It was meet that we should make merry, and be glad: for this thy brother was dead, and is alive again; and was lost, and is found. (Luke 15: 11-32)*

10. *Orthodox Dogmatic Theology, written by Fr. Michael Pomazansky, translated by Fr. Seraphim Rose*
    The Orthodox Church, written by Timothy Ware

11. *"We cannot partake deeply in the life of God unless we change profoundly. It is therefore essential that we should go to God in order that He should transform and change us, and that is why, to begin with, we must all become converts. Conversion in Latin and Hebrew means a turn, a change in the direction of things. The Greek word … means a change of mind.*

    Conversion means that instead of spending our lives looking in all directions, we should follow one direction only. It is a turning away from a great many things that we know are ultimately not good for us. The first impact of conversion is to modify our sense of values: God being at the center of all, everything acquires a new position and a new depth. All that is God's; all that belongs to Him is positive and real. Everything that is outside of him ultimately has no value or meaning.

175

But it is not change of mind alone that we can call conversion. We can change our minds and go no further: what must follow is an act of will and unless our will comes into motion and is redirected towards God, there is no conversion; at most there is only an incipient, still dormant and inactive change in us.
Metropolitan Anthony of Surozh

12. *The Acquisition of the Holy Spirit in Ancient Russia, by I.M. Kontzevitch, pg. 11*

13. *"In the Mystery of Repentance the spiritual afflictions of a man are treated, impurities of soul are removed, and a Christian, having received forgiveness of sins, again becomes innocent and sanctified, just as he came out of the waters of Baptism. Therefore, the Mystery of Repentance is called a 'spiritual medicine.' One's sins, which draw a man downward, which dull his mind, heart and conscience, which blind his spiritual gaze, which make powerless his Christian will – are annihilated, and one's living bond with the Church and with the Lord God is restored. Being relieved of the burden of sins, a man again comes to life spiritually and becomes able to strengthen himself and become perfected in the good Christian path."* Dogmatic Theology, pg. 287

14. *Your Godparents pray for you for their entire life. When you are a child, they bring you to your first Holy Communion. They are yet other guardians that watch over your soul.*

15. *"**The Fall**"*
    [1] Now the serpent was more subtle than any beast of the field, which the LORD God had made. And he said unto the woman, Yea, hath God said, ye shall not eat of every tree of the garden?
    [2] And the woman said unto the serpent, We may eat of the fruit of the trees of the garden:
    [3] But of the fruit of the tree which is in the midst of the garden, God hath said, ye shall not eat of it, neither shall ye touch it, lest ye die.
    [4] And the serpent said unto the woman, Ye shall not surely die:
    [5] For God doth know that in the day ye eat thereof, then your eyes shall be opened, and ye shall be as gods, knowing good and evil.
    [6] And when the woman saw that the tree was good for food, and that it was pleasant to the eyes, and a tree to be desired to make one wise, she

took of the fruit thereof, and did eat, and gave also unto her husband with her; and he did eat.

[7] And the eyes of them both were opened, and they knew that they were naked; and they sewed fig leaves together, and made themselves aprons.

[8] And they heard the voice of the LORD God walking in the garden in the cool of the day: and Adam and his wife hid themselves from the presence of the LORD God amongst the trees of the garden.

[9] And the LORD God called unto Adam, and said unto him, Where art thou?

[10] And he said, I heard thy voice in the garden, and I was afraid, because I was naked; and I hid myself.

[11] And he said, Who told thee that thou wast naked? Hast thou eaten of the tree, whereof I commanded thee that thou shouldest not eat?

[12] And the man said, The woman whom thou gavest to be with me, she gave me of the tree, and I did eat.

[13] And the LORD God said unto the woman, What is this that thou hast done? And the woman said, The serpent beguiled me, and I did eat.

[14] And the LORD God said unto the serpent, Because thou hast done this, thou art cursed above all cattle, and above every beast of the field; upon thy belly shalt thou go, and dust shalt thou eat all the days of thy life:

[15] And I will put enmity between thee and the woman, and between thy seed and her seed; it shall bruise thy head, and thou shalt bruise his heel.

[16] Unto the woman he said, I will greatly multiply thy sorrow and thy conception; in sorrow thou shalt bring forth children; and thy desire shall be to thy husband, and he shall rule over thee.

[17] And unto Adam he said, Because thou hast hearkened unto the voice of thy wife, and hast eaten of the tree, of which I commanded thee, saying, Thou shalt not eat of it: cursed is the ground for thy sake; in sorrow shalt thou eat of it all the days of thy life;

[18] Thorns also and thistles shall it bring forth to thee; and thou shalt eat the herb of the field;

[19] In the sweat of thy face shalt thou eat bread, till thou return unto the ground; for out of it wast thou taken: for dust thou art, and unto dust shalt thou return.

[20] And Adam called his wife's name Eve; because she was the mother of all living.

[21] Unto Adam also and to his wife did the LORD God make coats of skins, and clothed them.

[22] And the LORD God said, Behold, the man is become as one of us, to know good and evil: and now, lest he put forth his hand, and take also of the tree of life, and eat, and live for ever:

[23] Therefore the LORD God sent him forth from the Garden of Eden, to till the ground from whence he was taken.

[24] So he drove out the man; and he placed at the east of the Garden of Eden Cherubims, and a flaming sword, which turned every way, to keep the way of the tree of life. (Genesis, chapter 3)

16. *Streams of Inspiration, Monastery of St. John of San Francisco, vol.1, issue 3*

17. *The Life of Mary, The Theotokos (Greek for Mother of God), written and compiled by Holy Apostles Convent (See Appendix I, The Life of Mary, for my Reader's Digest version of the early life of Mary.)*

18. *The Orthodox Veneration of Mary, The Birthgiver of God, by St. John Maximovitch, St. Herman of Alaska Press*

19. *From the hymn "All of Creation" sung during Lent on Sundays*

20. *Fasting from foods such as meat, dairy, seafood and/or oil is a traditional practice during the year in the Orthodox Church. There are fasting seasons such as Advent, which precedes Christmas, Great Lent, which precedes Pascha or Easter, the Dormition Fast, which precedes the feast of the repose of the Mother of God, and the Apostles Fast, which follows Pentecost. These fasts are two to seven weeks long. Orthodox Christians also generally fast on Wednesdays and Fridays in honor of the Crucifixion, except when we have a "fast-free" week.*

The strictness with which one personally approaches and participates in the fasting process depends upon one's state of health and mind and the support of one's pastor, confessor or spiritual father or mother. We are also asked to refrain from worldly distractions:

television, movies and sexual relations, and most importantly, from our negative passions for a season or a day. "Your heart shall live that seek God." (Ps. 69:32) Fasting becomes an opportunity to turn to God and learn how to indwell in the Holy Spirit.

21. *Kontakion from the Great Canon by St Andrew of Crete, Lenten Triodion*

22. **More from St. Theophan and Veronica about the three aspects of the soul.**

"These are the noetic, active and sensual aspects of the soul. St. Theophan states that the human soul because it is inspired with the spirit of God is always yearning for the ideal. The manifestations of our yearnings for this ideal differ greatly depending upon which realm is directing our soul, the fallen or the Godly.

In addition, according to St. Theophan, the intellect (noetic aspect) of our soul is guided by experience and observation. From what it learns from its experiences, our soul draws conclusions and obtains suppositions about how things are and work. However, most of this noetic activity of the soul is accomplished haphazardly and disconnectedly.

*The **active part** of our soul is motivated by the desire to do good and the production of unselfish deeds. Our soul actively seeks what will satisfy the needs of our temporal life in its lower state, but St. Theophan notes that this will never be enough to ensure the soaring of our spirit towards God unless we unselfishly do good and help others. Selfless, virtuous actions are often not pleasant or monetarily beneficial to us. In the higher spiritually active aspect of our soul we can accomplish extraordinary things for others with little or any regard for our wellbeing. The more virtuous our actions, the more we acquire the Holy Spirit, the more our souls soar."*

The lower expression of this active part of my soul I could sense was driven by different desires: the approval and love of others, the desire for money, wanting to be the best, or even running away from some hidden fear. I could see how often my unconscious desires to make a difference were actually not motivated at all by virtue, but self-interest disguised as wanting to do good for others.

*"In the **sensual part** of the soul, there appears a yearning and love for the beautiful." St. Theophan refers to the lower aspect of our senses as mercenary and solely interested in self-gratification. The higher*

aspect of the sensual aspect of our soul is motivated by our delight in what is beautiful. When in this higher aspect of our soul's senses - we are touched by beauty - we do not grab for it. We have a need for order and beauty in our homes. Our enjoyment of nature, good music, art and books helps us to connect with something greater than ourselves.
A Spiritual Life, pg. 48

23. *A Spiritual Life, pg. 66-71*

24. *Dispassion is "passionlessness, the uprooting of the passions… or dispassion signifies a state in which the passions are exercised in accordance with their original purity and so without committing sin in act or thought." The Philokalia*

25. *The Orthodox Church does not place the same emphasis on Christ's suffering for and because of our sins as the Western Catholic Church. Rather, the Eastern Church believes Christ died to free us from sin and death. For when sin entered the world, so did death.*

    "Let us enter into the meaning of the mystery of the Cross … The world, that is the human race, would have been given over to eternal death … if the son of God had not become, out of his limitless goodness, a voluntary Intermediary and Redeemer of mankind, which was … corrupted by sin. For, by the deception of the serpent, the murderer of men, it was cast down into a frightful abyss … However, so that men might be capable of this reconciliation and redemption from above, it was necessary for the Son of God to descend into the world, to take upon Himself a human soul and body, and become the God-Man, in order that in his own Person, in His human nature, He might fulfill all the righteousness of God, which had been brazenly violated by all manner of human unrighteousness, in order that He might fulfill the whole of the Law of God, even to the least iota, and become the greatest of righteous men for the whole of unrighteous mankind, and teach mankind righteousness with repentance for all its unrighteousness and how forth the fruits of repentance. This He fulfilled, not being guilty of a single sin, and was the only perfect man, in hypostatical union with Divinity.
    Sermon on the Feast of the Exaltation of the Cross: "The Meaning of the Mystery of the Cross." St. John of Kronstadt

26. *St. John Damascus writes that the nous is the purest part of the soul, it is the eye of the soul. Orthodox Psychotherapy, Pg 119*

27. *Veneration of icons, The Orthodox Church by Timothy Ware, pg. 30-32*

28. *"The Son of Man must suffer many things…" Mk 8:31 Greater love hath no man but this, that a man lay down his life for his friends. Jn 15:13 "Father… not my will, but thine be done." Lk 22:42 as he wept tears of blood the night before his voluntary crucifixion. Through parables he confronted the Jewish elders with his power to lay down his life and to raise it up again, "Destroy this temple and in three days I will raise it up." Jn 2:18*

29. *The centurion's name was Longinus. He became a believer after witnessing Christ's Death. He was martyred for his witnessing and is now a saint.*

30. *The Lamentations, an inspiring and beautiful service held on Holy Friday evening, which expresses the lamentations of the Mother of God and all creation at the Death of Christ while stirring within us the miracle of Christ's Voluntary death and approaching Resurrection.*

31. *Matins, service of Holy Saturday*

32. *Paschal Matins verse*

33. *"Make the heart of this people fat, and make their ears heavy, and shut their eyes; lest they see with their eyes, and hear with their ears, and understand with their heart, and convert, and be healed." Is 6:10*

34. *Let All Mortal Flesh, cherubic hymn sung on Holy Saturday*

35. *The Lamb is the term used for the sacred bread prepared for the chalice. Special prayers are recited over it throughout the service, including prayers for all the faithful parish members.*

36. ***A Grace Filled Awakening***
Sensing life with God in eternal bliss versus "bursts of exalted yearnings".
"During a grace-filled awakening the heart is allowed to sense another better, more perfect, joyous life. This, However, is not at all

what people have who feel an awakening of bright impulses and noble yearnings (which we call a movement of ideas). These manifestations correspond to that which is exalted over the ordinary order of things and tend toward the realization of the grace-filled suggestion, but they diverge widely in direction and goals. The latter push one into some sort of foggy area, while the first turn one to God, show the peace that is in Him, and grant a foretaste of it. The goal of the first is life with God in eternal bliss, and of the latter it is 'something'. Of course, it is always something great and extraordinary, but nothing more can be said about it other than it is 'something'. The supreme difference between them is that the latter sort of burst in and act uniquely – the spirit inspires one person from one side and another person from another side, but the first embraces the entire spirit on all sides and placing it near the goal, satisfies it, or gives it a foretaste of the total satisfaction to come.

Bursts of exulted yearning are essentially traces of God's image in man; it is a shattered image, and therefore it is discovered as resembling splintered and scattered rays. These rays must be gathered into one and concentrated, and this focus creates an igniting ray. This, shall we say, concentrated ray of spirit, unified within itself but broken up within the many-faceted soul, produces the grace that awakens the soul and ignites the spiritual life – not by setting the person into cold contemplation, but into a certain life-producing burning. Such a gathering of spirit corresponds to the feeling of Divinity – this is embryonic life. It is the same in nature: life does not appear until its powers act in a shattering way; but as soon as the higher powers collect into one, a living existence is manifest – as, for example, in a plant. So it is in the spirit. While its impulses are breaking things up, now this and now that, now in this direction and now in that direction there is no life in it. When the higher, divine power of grace concurrently descends upon the spirit, it brings all of its strivings into one and holds them in this unity – then comes the fire of spiritual life.

By these signs it is easy to distinguish grace-filled awakening from ordinary manifestations of spiritual life, in order that they may not be confused, and mainly, in order not to miss the chance to make use of them for salvation. It is particularly necessary to know this regarding those times when the grace of God acts without any preliminary effort on the person's part, or without any particular strength. The awakened state cannot go by unnoticed, but it is possible to not give it the attention it deserves and, having been some time in it, again to fall into the ordinary circular motion of soul and body.

Awakening does not complete the work of the sinner's conversion, but only initiates it; the work on himself lies ahead and is very complicated work at that. Everything, by the way, related to this is completed in two turning points: first in the movement toward oneself, and then away from oneself to God. By the first movement the person regains the authority he had lost over himself, and the second brings him forth as a sacrifice to God – a whole-burnt offering of freedom. In the first movement he comes to the decision to abandon sin, and in the second, drawing nearer to God, he gives a promise to belong to Him alone throughout the days of his life."

The Path to Salvation, St Theophan the Recluse, pg 151-53

37. The Misuse of Mindfulness

"Here we are treading on dangerous ground, so it is necessary to step lightly. This is where many who have practiced watchfulness have fallen into delusion over the centuries. Everything depends on the purity of one's intention in going within. If one's intention (conscious or unconscious) is not to face one's sin-condition, repent and thus be reconciled to God, but instead to be "spiritual" while continuing to worship oneself, then one can - upon becoming aware of the light of one's spirit - begin to worship it as God. This is the ultimate delusion."

"Archimandrite Sophrony writes: "Attaining the bounds where 'day and night come to an end,' man contemplates the beauty of his own spirit which many identify with Divine Being. They do not see a light but it is not the True Light in which there is 'no darkness at all.' It is a natural light peculiar to the mind of man created in Gods image."

"The mental light, which cells every other light of empirical knowledge, might still just as well be called darkness, since it is the darkness of divestiture and God is not in it. And perhaps in this instance more than any other we should listen to the Lords warning, 'take Keith there for that the light which is in you been out darkness.' The first prehistoric, cosmic catastrophe – the fall of Lucifer – son of the morning, who became the prince of *darkness — was due to his enamored contemplation of his own beauty, which ended up in his self- deification."*

"The darkness of divestiture of which Fr. Sophrony speaks is the state of having risen above all thoughts and thought processes, which we have described earlier. If a person's motive is prideful, he will stop at this point, admiring his own brilliance; but that brilliance will still be darkness. He will think he has found God, but God will not be there. He will find a kind of peace, but it will be a piece apart from God."

"To go beyond thought is not yet to attain true knowledge. Since knowledge comes from the Word speaking wordlessly in the spirit that is yearning for Him; it does not come from the spirit itself. The Word will come and make His abode in the spirit only if the person approaches Him an absolute humility, for He Himself is humility, and like attracts like."

"Fr. Sophrony writes further on those who go within themselves without humility: "Since those who enter for the first time into the sphere of the 'silence of the mind' experience a certain mystic awe, they mistake their contemplation for mystical communion with the Divine, whereas in reality they are still within the confines of created human nature. The mind, it is true, here passes beyond the frontier of time and space, and it is this that gives it a sense of grasping eternal wisdom. This is as far as human intelligence can go along the path of natural development and self-contemplation..."

"Dwelling in the darkness of divestiture, the mind knows a particular delight and sense of peace.... Clearing the frontiers of time, such contemplation approaches the mind to knowledge of the intransitory, thereby possessing men of new but still abstract cognition. Woe to him who mistakes this wisdom for knowledge of the true God, and this contemplation for a communion in Divine Being. Woe to him because the darkness of divestiture on the borders of true vision becomes an impenetrable pass and a stronger barrier between himself and God than the darkness which results from the loss of grace and abandonment by God. Woe to him, for he will have gone astray and fallen into delusion, since God is not in the darkness of divestiture."

Christ the Eternal Tao, Hieromonk Damascene, pgs. 327

Other Books Published by Veronica Hughes

The sequel to *The Pearl of Great Price*
Available in Paperback and Kindle Version on Amazon
For an autographed copy go to: thepearlofgreatpriceorthodox.com

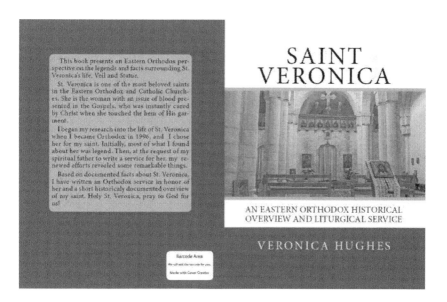

Available in on Amazon
For an autographed copy go to: thepearlofgreatpriceorthodox.com

Made in the USA
Middletown, DE
01 October 2022

11492943R00120